Praise for
Discovering Unexpected Gifts

"With an engaging, immediate writing style, Stephen Now shows us a harmonious interplay between the twists and turns of his life path and his capacity to find gratitude, personal growth, and humility around every corner. In taking this reflective journey with him, we, in turn, are offered the opportunity to reflect on our own lives through the same appreciative lens. Ultimately, what Stephen offers us is the opportunity to see that gifts arrive not just in the form of obvious gains, but through loss, hardship, and setback as well."

—Kerry Ragain, Ph.D.

"This book is a gift. As the author leads us through his life's events identifying the gifts they brought and lessons learned, we can't help but be inspired to do the same with our own."

—Cheryl Manriquez, Social Worker

"An honest, heartfelt, and reflective memoir of a loving and compassionate therapist whose ability to bear witness without judgment and to impact and be impacted by the clients and individuals he meets along his life journey while teaching and learning life lessons in sometimes unexpected and messy ways. Just what the world needs in 2021!"

—Liana Montague, Child and Family Therapist

Discovering Unexpected Gifts

In the Midst and Through the Chaos of Life

Stephen Now

Made for Success Publishing
P.O. Box 1775 Issaquah, WA 98027
www.MadeForSuccessPublishing.com

Copyright © 2021 Stephen Now

All rights reserved.

In accordance with the U.S. Copyright Act of 1976, the scanning, uploading, and electronic sharing of any part of this book without the permission of the publisher constitutes unlawful piracy and theft of the author's intellectual property. If you would like to use material from the book (other than for review purposes), prior written permission must be obtained by contacting the publisher at service@madeforsuccess.net. Thank you for your support of the author's rights.

Distributed by Made for Success Publishing

First Printing

Library of Congress Cataloging-in-Publication data
Stephen Now
      Discovering Unexpected Gifts: In the Midst and Through the Chaos of Life
         p. cm.

      LCCN: 2021934489
      ISBN: 978-1-64146-628-8 (*Paperback*)
      ISBN: 978-1-64146-670-7 (*Audiobook*)
      ISBN: 978-1-64146-629-5 (*eBook*)

Printed in the United States of America

For further information contact Made for Success Publishing +14255266480 or email service@madeforsuccess.net

Contents

Foreword 7

Introduction 13

Part One
Unexpected Gifts

The gift of nurture 23
The gift of being taught 27
The gift of being seen and believed in 31
The gift of questioning 37
The gift of telling the truth 41
The gift of second chances 47
The gift of mentors 51
The gift of ambition… 59
…And the gift of failure 65
The gift of the unexpected 69
The gift of starting over 75
The gift of belonging 79
The gift of "yes" 83
The gift of presence 87

The gift of suddenly having your world shaken	93
The gift of closed doors	97
The gift of witnessing our humanity	101
The gift of supporting each other	107
The gift of powerlessness	111
The children	115
The gift of unconditional love	125
The gift of taking a hard look at how I've affected others and making amends	129

Part Two
Reflections

There is pain and suffering that cannot be called an "unexpected gift"	135
Some thoughts on living, giving, and receiving unexpected gifts	141
Some thoughts on chaos and order	153
Psalm 139:1-18 (ESV)	157

Foreword

> "We don't meet people by accident. They are meant to cross our path for a reason."
>
> —Unknown

Twenty years ago, a stranger walked into my life in South Africa. I was the first black CEO in the 140-year existence of the Cape Town YMCA—a non-profit program and facility serving youth and children. It was only a few years after South Africa became a democratic country when black South Africans started to come to terms with newfound freedom and "learn" to trust other people of color—especially white South Africans.

Enter Stephen, a white American wanting to know more about the work of our organization. Given the history of our country, I was understandably apprehensive and skeptical about his visit. That initial fear soon disappeared when I talked to him and realized that he had a genuine interest in what we were doing. He wasn't there to take pictures and never be seen again like many foreign visitors that visited our organization before.

His next few days were not spent soaking up the sun on Cape town's beautiful beaches or wine tasting at our world-renowned wine estates. On the contrary, he accompanied our volunteers visiting and interacting with young people and children in juvenile detention, schools, and community centers. In a very short time, the stranger became a friend, and per the title of this book, together, we started to *Discover the Unexpected Gifts* that his arrival would bring. Our meeting was not an accident but one of purpose and destiny.

Reading the book, you soon realize that this is not just any book but one with impact and meaning, a tapestry of events that will remind you of your life journey and how people, events, and experiences have impacted our lives.

In the chapter "The Gift of Nurture," we read about Mrs. Arney's long silver hair and lemon meringue pie. Growing up in apartheid South Africa, I saw communities formed by forced removals where people were dumped in townships; I also had a "Mrs. Arney" who took care of me while my parents were at work. Her name was Aunt Jeanette. She also had gray hair, but it was not lemon meringue pies that drew me but her cakes. More importantly, like in Stephen's case, she provided me with life essentials that kept me out of trouble. Similarly, most of us can identify with a Mrs. Arney or Aunty Jeannette who positively impacted our lives and kept us on the right track.

A question arose for me in the chapter "All About Me"; how many of us have fallen into the trap of chasing ambition without thinking about the consequences? Most of the decisions I have made in this case ended up in failure and heartsore, similar journeys we have made during our upbringing. Those hurdles shaped our lives and turned us into the adults we are today. The author's experience in this chapter is proof that an "all about me" attitude often leads to failure. The embarrassment of stumbling into the wrong delivery room because he got "buzzed" after drinking while waiting in the father's lounge was soon replaced with the joy of the birth of his first child. At just 21, this new dad realized that he had to first apologize for stumbling into the wrong delivery room and second to ask for directions before he could experience the excitement of seeing his son for the first time. What a life lesson; when you make a mistake, ask for forgiveness and then for direction or "correction" to experience success.

"From the Basement Up" describes the failures we have all tasted after a period of success. Some of us got up with scratches, others bruises, and proverbial broken bones in severe cases. However, success was not in our failure but in our ability to get up and try again.

In "The Gift of Starting Over," the author indicates not to worry about pleasing the "crowd." What's important is *who* is listening. The crowd was gone, but the school president was listening and giving his approval. Sometimes we need to move our lives to the basement to nurture our gifts and talents before we can climb the stairs to the top. It's in the basement where we practice and get better.

"The Gift of Presence." Wow! Sometimes you get so busy, preoccupied with your problems, not realizing that your healing process is in the people around you. Finding yourself in a place like Fircrest where you can be at home, being around people who don't see your faults and problems, you will experience healing when you allow others into your life and allow them to hold your pain or hurt or loss. This takes away the power of that pain, hurt, or loss, allowing you to experience peace.

Discovering Unexpected Gifts is about the author's life journey, but it's also about us—you, and me. It is a reminder about what shaped our life and an encouragement to never give up on our dreams and desires. But more importantly, to never give up on others, especially the vulnerable.

In our African culture, there is a word called Ubuntu. Ubuntu means "I am because you are." Ubuntu is part of the Zulu phrase "Umuntu ngumuntu ngabantu," which means that a person is a person through other people. Ubuntu has its roots in African humanist philosophy, where the idea of community is one of the building blocks of society. Ubuntu is that nebulous concept of common humanity, oneness: humanity, you and me both. Stephen is truly an example of the Ubuntu spirit. The chapters and stories are an indication that we are all connected, and the things that happen to us contribute to our development. I am who I am today because of Stephen and the many other individuals who have crossed my path during my lifetime.

> Llowellyn Syce, Principal, Breede Valley School of Skills Vaardigheidskool, Rawsonville, South Africa

Introduction

I have reached a place where I have started to realize that events throughout my life have a common thread—although each life event has offered quite unique experiences. The common thread, however, is that each experience has been a gift in its own unique way. A life-changing, eye-opening, heart-transforming gift.

Of course, I didn't realize it in the moment. Time, distance, and reflection have brought me the greatest gift of all—seeing the thread that runs through each of those life experiences for the first time.

Years ago, I went to a weekend retreat at a Catholic monastery. We were given the warm, hooded robes worn by the priests living there and participated in matins and vespers. Our facilitator spoke of a theme for the weekend entitled "Tapestries."

We were asked to complete a chart with vertical and horizontal columns. At the top of each vertical column, we placed the following experiences:

WORLD NEWS/EVENTS
MUSIC
MOVIES
BOOKS
RELATIONSHIPS
EDUCATION
OTHER EVENTS

And in the horizontal columns, we indicated different time periods in our lives:

CHILDHOOD
ADOLESCENCE
YOUNG ADULT
EDUCATION
EMPLOYMENT
MARRIAGE

We were then asked to fill in the empty spaces in each column with specifics relating to the headings. The assignment brought lots of discussions of "Oh, I haven't thought about that for years!" or "Do you remember so and so?"

When we were done, our group members were asked to share any thoughts or insights that occurred to them from their completed charts. Many noted major world events that had affected all of us, and often, turning points in people's lives were seen as a result of particular experiences.

Introduction

The facilitator concluded with a reading from the retreat theme, and the message was eye-opening. What looks ordered and defined on the front of the tapestry looks quite chaotic and disconnected on the backside, which is oft unseen. But that supposed chaos is what created the beauty. The same can hold true for us. Life's chaos is in our faces every day. We can't avoid its domination of our lives that seems so random and often cruel. And from our limited vantage point, we cannot find any sense of meaning or purpose or beauty or love. What was happening behind the scenes, however, was weaving something quite amazing bit by bit—*ourselves.*

This is a book about you. Although I am using my own experiences to share what has shaped (and continues to shape) who I am, it is only a referent for reflecting on *your* life experiences.

I find it astonishing that the message each and every one of us is given from the get-go is "not good enough." We will experience it through rejection or indifference, being told in countless different ways we need to be something or someone other than just ourselves to achieve freedom from this replayed message. We will hear it from those who came before us, carrying their own messages of "not good enough." We will be coerced, pushed, cajoled, and manipulated into giving ourselves away that we might be "good enough."

We may be fortunate to have loving, caring parents—but they are no match for the pressures beyond them. Like automatons, we step on the treadmill and run, run, run with degrees and careers and credit ratings and the "right" clothes, hair, body shape, car, home, love life, and social media presence.

This is a book for you to be with yourself, listen to yourself, care for yourself, and take risks for yourself. This is a book about truly accepting yourself as essentially worthy, of being amazed at how absolutely necessary and needed you really are. And you won't be doing it alone. Instead, you will become increasingly aware of the tapestry unfolding before you. This is about a larger view—a view discovering meaning, worth, and purpose. I would ask you to take notes of memories that surface for you as you read.

It's time.

Perhaps you've heard some version of the farmer and son story. I learned it as "Mebbe, mebbe not." As events keep occurring to the farmer and his son, the neighbors keep decrying their bad luck or exclaiming their great fortune. However, the farmer's consistent reply refuses to assign a value or a loss: "Mebbe, mebbe not." There's a bigger picture to consider. I often have been "the neighbors," concluding that my life was ruined or having what I thought was a success only to realize it was anything but.

The people who have come and gone in my life stay with me. What they said and did, how they cared and confronted, what they taught, how they hurt, and how I hurt them all bring me to this day with a sense of wonder, humility, gratitude, and desire to be someone who is there for others.

My chapters are short, more as glimpses of particular moments that were given to me and stay with me—and perhaps with *you* as you recognize similar experiences in your life. One day, a woman colleague I worked with in advocating for children in foster care seeking adoption said to me, "Who is invisible to you?" I was a bit taken aback at the blunt question. But boy, did it stay with me.

Who do I not see on city streets, in nursing homes, in school playgrounds, in impoverished neighborhoods, in line at the grocery store? Who do I not see who doesn't look like me or speak my language well?

Hopefully, I did truly "see" the people who came in and out of my life as I recount their stories in this writing. I am eternally grateful. They created my own life tapestry giving me meaning, value, and gratitude.

Just one week yet worlds apart

In 2018, I became a volunteer CASA—an acronym for Court Appointed Special Advocate. My work focused on being the eyes and ears for dependency court judges, giving reports and testimony on the circumstances of a child brought into social services protection. I also was given the responsibility of being "the voice" for the child, informing the judge what they wanted and what they needed.

In my process of gathering information, I met with a family member to seek their input. We hit it off almost immediately as we talked over coffee. In our conversation, I learned that we were all but one week apart in age—his birthday falling in August, mine in September. As we talked of common memories, world events, and experiences, it became increasingly clear that we experienced life in two very different tracks even though we were only one week apart. I grew up in an all-white middle-class neighborhood, while he grew up in an all-minority, gang-ruled neighborhood. I didn't think a thing about roaming around my neighborhood looking for someone to play with. He took his first bullet in the leg at age 5. I survived by getting good grades. He survived by being as tough a kid as he could be.

I was accepted at my parents' college with scholarships, and my draft order was deferred. He was recruited in the ROTC and immediately shipped to Vietnam. I completed my bachelor's and master's degree with student loans and grants. He returned having been seriously injured by a grenade that would hamper his ability to function the rest of his life. He lived in constant pain and became dependent on pain medications. I never knew life-threatening trauma. He dealt with PTSD through continued counseling and support groups. I became a counselor.

I tell this because of the absolute inequity of our two paths. But is that not a value judgment of what is good/bad, favorable/unfavorable, fair/unfair? The last time we had coffee together, he shared with me his dream of having a school strictly for African American boys that focused solely on their self-esteem, taking pride in who they are, and challenging any boundaries that kept them from their absolute highest potential.

The truth is, I wouldn't have known how to survive in the neighborhood he grew up in. He did. I don't believe if I had been sent to Vietnam that I would have survived. He did. And I don't know what it's like to muster the strength and courage he demonstrates each day of his life dealing with the pain year after year from past war injuries. He does.

Meeting this unexpected family member was a gift for me. I only hope my presence, my listening, and my appreciation was as much a gift for him as his was for me.

Part One
Unexpected Gifts

The gift of nurture

Mrs. Arney's long silver hair and the lemon meringue pie

As an only child of a fundamentalist, evangelical minister, I spent a good part of my life alone. My life revolved around the church's three services a week (two on Sunday and one on Wednesday evening), plus the many activities of Bible school, church camps, and revivals where special ministers called evangelists would preach eternal hellfire and brimstone until one got right with God. That meant long, drawn-out altar calls to come forward and give one's life to Jesus. I knew all these events as the sum of my life, tagging along as my parents saved sinners as their one and only "God-given" priority.

Being with other kids was a rarity—usually just kids whose parents went to my parents' church. And that gave me a label—preacher's kid. Preacher's kids got one of two definitions. Either they were "goody-two-shoes," or they were "little hellions." I'm not sure why, but somehow, I ended up with the latter reputation. I never really got the joke, but my dad would laugh that he had to give me a spanking every Sunday after church. Only I do remember it wasn't a spanking. It was a *whipping*. I still have memories as early as the first grade of pleading with my dad not to use his belt on me. I look back and wonder what a six-year-old could have done to warrant that. And I wondered why my mom stood by silently.

But someone did notice. Her name was Mrs. Arney. When my parents would travel to church conventions or district meetings, I stayed with Mrs. Arney. She was like an angel to me. I was treated with incredible kindness and warmth, as if I was the most special boy she had ever met. I had never known anything quite like it, and it was wonderful. I would follow around the house close behind her as she completed her household chores of the day, humming her favorite hymns.

"What is your favorite pie?" she asked as she worked in the kitchen one day. For some reason, I announced my favorite pie was lemon meringue. To this day, I'm still not sure exactly why I said that.

"Then you shall have a lemon meringue pie of your very own," she answered. And sure enough, as we finished lunch the next day, Mrs. Arney returned from the kitchen with a freshly baked lemon meringue pie. "You can eat as much as you like. This pie is just for you," she smiled. I took her offer literally. As she finished the dishes in the kitchen, I finished the entire pie. What followed was sheer misery and pain, followed by endless nausea all in one lemon meringue nightmare.

When my actions were discovered and my circumstances observed, Mrs. Arney set to work nurturing me back to health. I don't remember much more. But I do remember my vow never to touch another lemon meringue pie ever again (which I have kept to this day).

Mrs. Arney always had her hair in a bun. I'd never seen it any other way. But, as she was getting me ready for bed one evening, she removed some pins from her updo, and I watched as her silver and gray hair flowed all the way down her back. I was amazed. As she brushed her hair, I thought I'd never seen anyone quite so beautiful. It was a magical moment for me.

My parents would eventually move to another town, another church, and another congregation to save more souls in another community. But I never forgot Mrs. Arney. In fact, as I was about to leave for my parents' alma mater for my first year of college, I drove to her home just to be there one more time. She had been gone for some time. Someone else lived in that home now. But Mrs. Arney always lives in my heart. She was my first experience of kindness, love, and gentleness … and feeling like the most important boy in the world.

The gift of being taught

Teachers, teachers, teachers

Wow—where to start? What to say? If ever human beings have had a potential lifetime impact on other human beings, it's a pretty easy start to consider the teachers in our lives. Certainly, I am the evolved result of the powerful influences provided by the teachers who changed my life. And not all the "teachers" I am indebted to came from an academic setting.

I will start with the most unlikely but most powerful teaching moment in my life. After working several years as a child and family counselor for YMCA Family Services, I became increasingly aware of the devastating effects of AIDS in South Africa and decided to ask for a sabbatical to visit the Cape Town YMCA and volunteer wherever I could be useful. The director put me to work the second I arrived at the facility. Unlike the United States, YMCAs in South Africa are not "swim and gyms," but instead are entirely focused on volunteer programs for children and youth. Because of the number of deaths of parents and relatives caused by AIDS, hundreds if not thousands of children were left to survive on the streets. In a desperate response, the government was converting empty prisons into huge orphanages. Each day, YMCA volunteers would go to the prison/orphanages to teach. I was completely overwhelmed as I witnessed the conditions of these children for the first time. I stood with a social worker in one of the prison open spaces while we watched children exercise together. She told me she had 500 of those children on her caseload.

My role became one of caring for the volunteers as they approached burnout and being overwhelmed day after day. We would meet together to process what each had witnessed and created ways to support and care for each other.

I also visited the prison/orphanages daily and witnessed children sick and emaciated inside prison cells with unlocked doors.

I made arrangements with the director of the Cape Town YMCA to take a road trip to visit YMCAs around the country. Each place I arrived, I found the most amazing, gentle, and kind volunteers devoted to orphaned children. In Port Elizabeth, the children asked me to pick a song for all of us to sing. I started singing "This Little Light of Mine." In an instant, the song was transformed into the most joyous celebration sung by children at the top of their voices swaying to the rhythm and clapping their hands. They had become my teachers.

The gift of being taught

But my lesson for life was still yet to be experienced. As I traveled from region to region, I made every effort to stay in people's homes to make personal contact with families and learn more about their lives.

As I was completing the large circle I had made driving across the country, I arrived at a small town named Upington. After I found the residence where I would spend the night, I decided to take a walk to see the community and stretch my legs after a very long drive.

Walking through the residential area, I was approached by a young black man. His body was clearly malnourished. He held up two slippers barely held together by the remaining threads—each a different size. He asked, "Sir, would you happen to have an extra pair of shoes I could wear?"

I had packed light and only wore a pair of tennis shoes. "I'm sorry," I told him, "I can't help you." Without objection, he turned and walked away. But, as I returned to my room for the night, I realized I had a pair of sandals in my suitcase I hadn't even worn. I grabbed the sandals and began searching for the young man. Finally, I saw him sitting on the curb and began running to him. I watched his eyes grow large as I approached and realized I was frightening him. I stopped and held up the sandals. "Will these fit?" I asked. His eyes immediately lit up. I put the sandals in his hands, and he tried them on. They fit perfectly. I have never seen a face so full of joy! He laughed out loud, and we both stood together as he walked back and forth in his new shoes.

"Thank you, thank you," he kept repeating as he shook my hands over and overexpressing his gratitude. With a final "goodbye," I left for my room. I was unable to stop the tears that began to flow down my cheeks as I walked away.

Why was that one of my most significant life lessons? I'm not sure I can put that into words. But I do know that it changed me forever. I could never look at life quite the same way again. Indeed, I was the one who received the most unexpected gift that day.

The gift of being seen and believed in

A piano teacher named Nadine

Early on, my parents put their hopes in my becoming a pianist for the Billy Graham Crusades one day. I have no idea where that came from. My mother began giving me piano lessons as I turned six years old, and the mandated hours of daily practice became a part of my life. She played piano for all the church services and focused on my learning the hymns and choruses so I might follow in her footsteps.

But, at some point, she indicated I had surpassed her teaching skills, and we needed to find a professional teacher. The first attempt was an absolute bust. This teacher literally used a ruler when I was holding my hands in an incorrect position. And it hurt! Needless to say, I couldn't stand her and pleaded with my parents to find someone else.

Another ongoing pressure for my mastering the piano was the competition my parents seemed to have with another pastor and his family—all boys, and all talented musicians on trumpet playing together as a trio. Each year, the district of churches would hold a convention topped off with a talent contest for children and youth. I can't tell you how many times I sat through listening to a five-year-old in a cowboy outfit sing, "A Christian cowboy, a Christian cowboy, I'll ride for Jesus all day long."

The annual competition became my do or die against the horn-blowing Ketchum boys. I would perform on the grand piano. They would perform their trumpet arrangements. If I won the competition, the ride home was all smiles. If I lost, it was a silent one.

My most humiliating moment came when the annual event also fell at the same time as my contracting the flu. I lay miserably in the back seat of the car as we drove to the event, my mom assuring me I would feel better soon.

Then the moment came when we got past the "Christian Cowboys" and wiggly elementary school choirs, and my name was called for the final competition. Somehow, I made my way to the grand piano, adjusted the bench, and began playing. But, as I played, I couldn't control my bowels a minute longer and soiled myself. I finished the song, walked straight to the back of the church, and went to the car. It was locked. I can remember my parents coming out and, upon hearing of my predicament, begin arguing with each other about whose fault it was. That's all I remember. And that's when my parents contacted Nadine Clark.

Nadine Clark was well known in the classical music community and was in constantly high demand to take on the town's "brilliant youth" and teach them Bach and Beethoven, Franz Liszt and Schubert. And she was like nothing I had ever seen before. She was everything my parents preached against, and I immediately fell in love with her. She was thoroughly modern with her James Bond paperback collection, long cigarette holder (which she smoked while I played my lesson), bouffant hairstyle, and stylish '60s wardrobe.

And she had the most amazing grand piano I'd ever played. It was a Steinway—the Rolls Royce of pianos. Going from my daily spinet piano practices to her grand was like going to heaven once a week. I reveled in her correcting every little nuance of my recitals, expecting nothing but perfection from me. In fact, until Nadine gently advised me, I didn't realize that while I was playing, I was flapping my legs back and forth like I was taking off for flight.

Twice a year came the recitals for the parents—a major event for every one of her students. Her home was filled with folding chairs and tables covered with linens and delicate snacks. One by one, we took our turns doing our best at commanding the moment at that Steinway grand piano.

The unforgettable teaching moment for me came during one of my weekly recitals. As I was playing the assigned piece, I transitioned into one I had composed without making an indication of my shift. Nadine sat up from her sofa and asked, "What was that?" I thought for sure I would be scolded. But I wasn't.

"It's something I wrote," I softly replied.

"Play it again," she commanded. "I like it!" So, I did.

Each week I would bring something new that I had composed. Nadine Clark not only encouraged me; she mentored me. With each new composition, she provided feedback and suggestions I would have never learned on my own. After researching available songwriting award programs for students, she entered my compositions in competitions published around the country.

However, the event of all events was her contacting my high school choir director and telling me to take my song to him for his review. I was a junior in high school at the time and pretty much invisible. But things suddenly changed. My choir director decided to include my song in the choir's repertoire. And, at our next concert, my song was performed. Suddenly I was visible. Students who had never talked to me passed on kudos in the hallways. Teachers congratulated me. I ran for senior vice president and won.

After several more compositions were performed, Nadine Clark contacted the Seattle Opera and made arrangements for one of their soloists to perform my latest song for the school's spring concert with the full concert choir and orchestra. And *I* was asked to be the conductor.

The town's mayor was there, and the gymnasium was packed. I received a standing ovation at the close of the performance. Nadine Clark was there standing in the front row beaming. My life was changed forever thanks to Nadine Clark.

I said my goodbyes before heading to my first year of college unable to express how much she meant to me. I would never see her again. She had given me the biggest gift of my life—someone who saw me and believed in me.

The gift of questioning

Do you believe everything you read?

His name was Mr. Anderson—our new history teacher. Not only was he the newest teacher, but he was also the *youngest* teacher in our Navy yard town high school. He also came across as the most serious of all my teachers. I walked into his class expecting an hour of lecture and several more hours of assigned reading. But as the last of us wandered in, he closed the door, took roll call, and began …

"Do you believe everything you read?" he asked. "Do you think that history book you have on your desk tells the whole story of what transpired in the past? How do you decide if something you read is true or not? Do you believe the United States offers justice and fairness and equal opportunity for all of us? Do you believe the United States has treated other countries with respect and honesty? How did you come to those conclusions?"

The room was silent. "You can leave your book in your locker. Instead, bring a newspaper to class every day. We are going to read the news."

I found myself both excited and a little scared. I had never heard a teacher talk like this before. And yet, he was offering the very thing I wanted most—to be able to question what I had been told or read without fear.

Our class became a hub of discussions and disagreements and energy! Each of us would bring articles or stories that affected us, and methodically explored questions with the class, such as: Who is the source? What do we know about this source? What is the agenda, if any, of this report? Who has not been heard on this issue, this question? Who can't speak about what they see and what they experience? Why?

Mr. Anderson was teaching us to question and think critically. It was awesome. And he would call us on sloppy thinking or lack of research in presenting our positions. I looked forward to each day we reported to Mr. Anderson's class.

My enthusiasm unintentionally spilled over at home but was met with silence and clear disapproval. I later learned my father had gone to my high school to get me transferred out of Mr. Anderson's class. But the effort failed, much to my relief.

Mr. Anderson also was clear about patriotism—that looking critically at actions taken by a government isn't about trying to tear it down. It is about holding ourselves accountable to the values patriotism calls us to.

Our class of 1969 was witnessing a nation (and a world) in chaos and terror, and many of us would go to the very frontlines never to return or be the same again. Mr. Anderson gave us the gift of listening to oneself, seeking the bigger picture, choosing to speak up and challenge inequities and falsehoods. Mr. Anderson gave us the purpose and tools to move through the chaos with calm reflection and instilled values in us that will last a lifetime.

The gift of telling the truth

Kicked out of college

Thus far, I have mostly been sharing unexpected gifts that can be described as positive experiences—being noticed, being cared for, being mentored, and being exposed to larger views of life and the world.

But it would take a long time for me to recognize the gifts that, at the time, I saw as anything but meaningful.

As an adolescent shipped off to an Oklahoma Bible college to become indoctrinated into my parents' beliefs, I was angry. Really angry. And I was now powerless—submitted daily to the endless repeated messaging—chapel at the start of every day, prayers before each class, and required attendance at a mega-church next to the campus accommodating thousands every Sunday. It didn't take long to discover other students who also were in my situation, which quickly became the basis of alliances and friendships.

I began to lead a double life at school, not unlike my life growing up at home. I would present myself as what my parents wanted to see—and grew exceptionally good at doing what I wanted without any evidence for them to learn of my duplicity. When I did get caught, it was met with extreme consequences. So, I kept getting better.

The problem was, I didn't realize I was making a pattern for myself that would be the source of most of my pain in life. My knee-jerk reaction in all my relationships was duplicity. I had internalized being unable to truly show myself. I always needed an emergency exit. I would tell others what they wanted to hear and do what they wanted to do, and bit by bit, I gave myself away—only to exit and escape again.

During the day, I was the ideal student. Getting good grades, playing the piano for choir and student outreach performances, and being the good Christian student. Ironically, as time passed, I realized I was *not* alone. It was a campus full of hypocrisy. It seemed like everybody was playing some kind of duplicity game. And I became increasingly cynical and isolated.

I let my hair grow long, wore the same clothes day after day, and went through the motions without any investment in relationships or community. I then began doing drugs with students I had easily identified as being as disillusioned as I was.

The gift of telling the truth

With only the limited exposure to life growing up in a sheltered childhood and adolescence and now a suffocating, hypocritical organization, I couldn't see any future, any hope, anything to believe in.

My roommate had prescription medications in the room, and I decided to take them all. I woke up in a hospital with no idea how I got there. My roommate later told me he found me and called for help.

My dad arrived the next day and came directly to the hospital. When I was discharged, he drove us to my grandmother's empty house. She was now in convalescent care. Alone in the house, he confronted me. "Do you believe in God?" he asked as he stood in front of me.

"I don't know, Dad," I replied, looking down at his shoes. He asked again. "Do YOU believe in God?" Again, I replied, "I don't know." And then he began to swing his fists, punch after punch. I was so completely caught off guard; I wasn't sure how to respond. I just stood there. I couldn't hit my dad. So, I remained standing in front of him until he was exhausted and finally stopped.

I ran out of the house and made my way back to my campus and dorm room. He left the next day.

My actions brought me to the office of the dean of students. He wanted information. Who was breaking school rules? Who were the students using drugs? Did my roommate sell drugs on campus? I played ignorant and was dismissed.

I remained at school for another year, going to class, doing my assignments, and working part-time jobs. It was better than going home, and, honestly, I didn't have any other options. The one source of warmth and affection turned out to be my elderly grandmother living in convalescent care not far away. I would visit her regularly and find her delighted to see me. With a touch on my cheek, she would say, "Stephen, you need to get a haircut!" But it wasn't a scolding, just a tease and a smile.

I refused to go to the required morning chapel services or to Sunday mega-church services, which came to the notice of the Dean of Students and meant several hundred dollars in chapel fines. (Later, I would have to pay those fines to get transcripts for my admittance to Emerson College.)

And I met a girl. She, too, had grown up in similar circumstances, which made for an instant understanding of each other. She had a car, and we used that car to travel all over the place doing whatever we wanted. Eventually, we found a dirt-cheap apartment we could afford with our part-time jobs and moved off-campus.

I was advised by the Dean of Students that I would not be welcomed back the next fall. With that announcement, we

The gift of telling the truth

began a road trip back to Washington State, having absolutely no idea what we were doing.

So, what was the "gift" of surviving a time in my parents' evangelical Bible college and the loss of ever having anything but "safe," polite, meaningless conversations with my father for the rest of his life?

I told the truth. I didn't give the answer that would have pleased the most powerful person in my life. And I told the truth to myself in seeking out who I really was even if I didn't know what that meant yet.

I didn't strike back. My sense of what was right and wrong wouldn't allow me to strike my own father.

And, unexpectedly, I was given the gift of time with an elderly grandmother who I hadn't seen since childhood. She turned out to be the nurturer, listener, and kind voice that I knew meant love.

The gift of second chances

The taboo of sex and the confusion, oh— the confusion

One of the messages of my upbringing came from my parents' church's emphasis on being "holiness people"—not of "this world of sin and lust," but chaste, modest, and pure. Sex was about all kinds of sin. The result for my adolescent life was living in a world of confusing information—or none at all. I had no siblings to figure things out with. I was not allowed to go to school dances (rock music and touching lead to sin). I wasn't allowed to go to movies (immoral women in revealing clothes and lustful men). I wasn't allowed to listen to the radio if there was any hint of rock 'n roll music. My mother would actually take scissors to newspapers or magazines arriving at our home for any "inappropriate" material before I could read them. My television viewing was closely monitored, and shows like "Flipper" were not allowed because women characters wore swimsuits.

Discovering Unexpected Gifts

I remember my mom crying when she caught our pet beagles in heat going at it. And I remember our going on a camper vacation, eventually setting up camp beside a small lake. As my dad and I waited outside in our swim trunks, my mom stepped out of the camper wearing a modest swimsuit. She lasted about three minutes, turned around, rushed back into the camper crying, and slammed the door. That was the first and only time I ever saw her in anything but a full-length dress or bathrobe.

My dad certainly never brought up the topic. This led only to the increased effort on my part to learn what this was all about. I'm not going to go into all the embarrassing moments an adolescent boy with wrong information from peers can get into. What I will say is I believe this has been a challenge for many, if not all, of us in varying experiences growing up into adult life.

Without adult mentoring, listening, and talking openly, I came to believe that what I saw on television or in the movies was reality. The message played over and over again was two people finding "the one," the lover, partner, eternal soulmate finally discovered and immediately recognized as each stared into the other's eyes.

With that, I had a double whammy—shame for my feelings of sexuality and blindly bouncing from one encounter to another, desperately looking for what was a complete illusion. I once had someone who I was sure was "the one" say to me,

"You're not in love with me. You're in love with your idea of who you think I am." Ouch. She was right.

I am most grateful that life has a way of granting us second, third, fourth chances because, as far as I am concerned, I needed to learn from all those moments. Step by step, they began pointing me in the direction of:

1. Learning how to love myself, and
2. Learning how to love someone else.

With that realization comes, bit by bit, learning new life skills such as empathy, the ability to laugh at oneself, grace, playfulness, spontaneity, listening, talking things through, intimacy, enjoying a life together and continually getting to know one another not only as lovers, but as best friends. We become "the one" over a lifetime of shared struggles and challenges, tears and laughter, hard work and just having fun together, mutual respect, and deepening trust.

And THAT is the gift. And it is most precious.

The gift of mentors

The youngest newspaper publisher

Returning to my home state after being away at college for two years meant one single priority—making money. I was absolutely broke, driving a sputtering VW Beetle with no place to live other than returning to my old room at my parents' house. That was not an option. It's certainly debatable if I should look at this as another gift… but, on the way back from Oklahoma, my open U-Haul trailer containing all my belongings, covered and roped down with a canvas tarp, caught fire as I drove down the freeway. When I saw the flames in my rearview mirror, I hit the brakes and the blaze leaped straight up. I was able to disconnect the trailer hitch and drive my car away, watching in silence as the trailer and its contents burned down to charred remains.

There was nothing to do but drive on. However, I had bought insurance on the trailer, and that meant a thousand-dollar check when I made my claim. It was enough to rent a single-room apartment and buy some folding chairs and an inflatable bed cushion.

Looking for work was a hopeless daily effort, as Seattle was then in a recession. Finally, I was hired at minimum wage working in a phone room, trying to talk people into home repair or remodeling estimates from salespeople who I wouldn't even trust to come near my home. It was a miserable job, and I continued to apply daily to every employment ad I thought I might have a chance at getting hired.

I did have a pretty good knack at writing in school, and thought I'd like to take a shot at working for a newspaper. I applied at the larger dailies and didn't get a single bite. So, I moved on, trying my luck with smaller weekly newspapers. And I got a nibble—a small-town weekly in rural farm country.

At my interview, the owner/publisher/printing press operator/front desk receptionist (you get my drift) noted my going to a Bible college. He indicated he was a member of a similar denomination and offered me the job of editor. I saw no need to mention that I had been asked to leave that school. That and the fact that I had taken up the habit of smoking cigarettes and quickly realized I would need to conceal my transgressions since tobacco (and alcohol) were certainly not acceptable under any circumstances.

The gift of mentors

No more than a day after my starting as the new editor, a local patron walked into the lobby and asked my new boss if the "new guy" needed an apartment. I was introduced, taken to his basement apartment, shown around, asked a few background questions, and signed on the dotted line.

I had never lived in such a small town before and quickly came to realize this was indeed a different culture of everyone knowing everyone else's business—or at least *they* thought so. Gossip was the currency of the community. As I began my editing of the weekly editions, I was given columns on various women's club activities, Rotary Club fundraising carnivals, and meeting notices. I sat in on city council meetings, checked the police reports weekly, attended high school football games, and reminded readers to support the local library bake sale. I was quickly becoming immersed. And with my immersion came long hours and little sleep as that deadline had to be met every week.

Then suddenly, things came to a halt. My employer sat me down and announced he was closing down the paper. It had lost too much money for too many years, and he would need to make his living just running a print shop.

Carl Jung, a published and acclaimed psychiatrist, spoke of four stages in life: the athlete, the warrior, the diplomat, and the shaman. The athlete stage is all about developing one's strength and power. Moving to another referent point, we now know that the human prefrontal cortex (considered the more rational lobe) is not fully developed until about age 25. I had just turned 20. For some crazy reason, I believed I could become my own newspaper publisher. It was my time to claim my power. And I had no idea what I was doing nor how I would pull this off—but I went for it.

I approached my boss and offered to buy the newspaper. I was essentially faking it. I didn't have any means to make an offer, but I had an idea. I went back to all the merchants I would pick up weekly ads from each Monday and asked each of them if I were to buy the paper, what they need from me to get their business. The crucial merchant was the grocery store, which bought the biggest ads each week. The answer was unanimous: circulation. They wanted their ads seen by the most customers possible.

My break came with that grocery store chain. I asked the owner for an advance on his advertising for me to have some beginning cash flow. He countered by offering to create a limited partnership agreement, and we had a deal. What followed was a flurry of activity establishing the sale price, drawing up the sales agreement, moving equipment and furniture to a new office, and announcing to the world I now owned the town's weekly newspaper.

I was in WAY over my head. My life became one of working night and day, seven days a week. And I was in trouble—I couldn't do it all, and I couldn't afford to pay anyone but my one typesetter/receptionist/film developer/bookkeeper.

This is where my unexpected gift arrived. His name was Mike. He came to the office seeking an editor's position. His resume was outstanding—clearly more professional than I could ever afford. After reviewing his training and credentials, I handed the resume back to him, indicating my thanks for his coming in, but I would not be able to afford what he would be looking for in a salary. He responded by asking what would be affordable. I didn't want to embarrass myself with a real answer. Apologetically I asked, "Would a hundred bucks a week work for a while?"

"Yes, that would be fine for now. I've got some time before I can get a position working as a company representative in China," he answered.

My jaw dropped. "Are you sure? I wish I could pay more."

Mike worked right by my side, cutting my workload by more than half. We would each gather our materials—advertising for me, news reports for him—put the paper together, take it to the press, and deliver it to waiting delivery students and drivers week after week. He was at least 10 years my senior, and with each week, his influence taught me new ways of accomplishing my goals. Where my younger rash decisions or behaviors would have cost me dearly, he could smooth things down a notch or two to help me see the bigger picture. Although I was technically the employer, he was indeed my teacher. I witnessed his kindness, his warmth and humor, his patience, and his deep love for his wife and found myself looking up to him.

The paper was on its way. And, as a member of the Washington State Newspapers Association, I suddenly gained a bit of notoriety as I was dubbed the youngest newspaper publisher in the state's history.

A few months later, an unknown cartoonist came to our office asking for a chance to have his work published. We ran his work to much enthusiasm—that is, until he gained national recognition as the creator of "The Far Side." His name was Gary Larson. His first panels with us were named "Nature's Way."

The day I dreaded but knew would eventually come had arrived. Mike received an offer. He would be traveling to China as a representative of Weyerhauser Corporation. He was actually quite apologetic. All I could say was, "Go, go—this is your chance!" I believe it was a difficult parting for both of us. He had literally saved me from failing at something much bigger than I could ever have handled on my own. And with that, he quietly and gently mentored me, pointing to values and ways of living that now I fully embrace. (Although, admittedly, it took a while.)

The gift of mentors

It wasn't just that he saved my behind running a small-town weekly newspaper. He was more a messenger and model of much more important things than financial success or prestige. He was the gift I needed most—someone to model and teach me about what really matters in life. I have no idea where he is (I have tried finding him to no avail), and I'm not even sure if he is still living. But he has stayed with me throughout my life.

The gift of ambition...

"All about me"

It's time for me to take a pause here. Thus far, I've shared mostly about positive experiences with caring, thoughtful, and kind people coming and going in my life and leaving unexpected gifts with me. But to truly see the larger picture, unexpected gifts can sometimes be anything but pleasant. They can be jarring. They can be painful. They can be heartbreaking. And they can be a wake-up call.

I had what I would call an "interesting experience" with a cousin I hadn't seen for years, some years older than me, and like my father—an evangelical pastor. I was just getting established running my weekly newspaper when he came to my office during a visit to the area. I politely showed him around the operation and then returned to my office to wrap up his visit. He looked at me and said, "I am praying that God will place a ring of thorns around you."

At first, I was a bit taken aback by his closing statement, but then I was just pissed. He was using the same old shame, fear, and judgment line I had heard so many times in my life. But this one was different. I politely thanked him for stopping by and rushed him out the door.

It was all about me now. I put my every thought and effort into promoting my own interests. I was going to build my empire. I got the sports car. I got the clothes. I got the house on the hill. And my every moment was about what I wanted.

And then I came home to the news. I was going to be a father—a 21-year-old father.

My co-rebelling partner and I had founded a relationship on escaping the control and boundaries of our parents' lives. We completely blew them off on a wild ride of newly discovered freedom. But, as we became entrenched in a new life of responsibility, bills, running a business, and going to Rotary and Junior Women's Club meetings, the bond that brought us together became irrelevant and vanished. I was doing my thing. She was doing hers. And now, a completely dependent human being was about to become our sole responsibility.

This was real. This was having to reconnect with our parents, who were about to become grandparents. This meant the party was over and no more spur-of-the-moment wild rides into the future.

So, we began the process—appointments with the pediatrician, going to parenting classes, creating a room for the baby, smiling and nodding as we shared the news. But I was still focused on me. And I attempted to escape by working more and staying later, leaving everything up to her.

When the day arrived, we made our way to the local hospital, and I was told to remain in the waiting room. There were no fathers allowed in the delivery room at that time, even though we had participated in parenting classes. I sat with other expectant dads, waiting for *hours*. One of the fathers-to-be had brought a briefcase, and inside was every airline mini bottle of hard liquor you could imagine. I didn't really care much for alcohol, but I accepted the friendly offer of my peer. And I got buzzed. When I was told I could go back to the delivery room, I stumbled into the wrong room. Embarrassed, I apologized and asked for directions. And there they were—mother and child. As I was able to hold this tiny new life in my arms, I was overwhelmed, amazed, captivated, and falling in love all at the same time.

Life became a mother-in-law moving to town and increased contact with my parents. I became the one who pointed the way to the baby.

Discovering Unexpected Gifts

Fast forward five years. I was able to hire more staff, carry less responsibility on my shoulders, and was already looking for my next accomplishment. It came through my visit to an advertising agency seeking their business. I was introduced to an ad exec who worked with media, including radio and television. She noted using a recording studio that was producing major acts such as Heart, Marvin Gay, Crosby, Stills, and Nash, and I was immediately intrigued. I asked for the contact information and showed up at their door the next week.

As I met with the owner/producer, I asked questions about writing and creating my own album. He gave me some pointers and agreed he would review my songs when I was ready to present them. I couldn't believe my good fortune. Here was a chance to not just write music for high school choirs, but to have a shot at being a rock star. This guy had connections!

A few weeks later, I returned with my collection of songs and sat at the studio's grand piano. I had a dozen songs ready. As the producer listened, he would stop me with, "Next!" even though I had just got started. I was getting nervous and quite intimidated. After song number six, I moved to the next song to hear him say, "We can use that one." Then a thumbs up to five more.

We agreed to record those six songs with studio musicians backing me up. I left the studio walking on air. I could still recall my amazement at the middle school dance in the gym when the teacher put on the Beatles' "I Want to Hold Your Hand" and every girl in the facility began screaming completely out of control. Yep—I was going to be a rock star.

...And the gift of failure

"Rock star, rock schmuck"

It's a continually humbling experience to realize that what you thought you wanted wasn't what you wanted at all. In my efforts to redefine myself as a famous recording artist, I actually lost myself—step-by-step. Yes, I was successful in writing, recording my own songs, creating albums, and developing my skills as a musician and songwriter. But I was absolutely blind to the realities I was creating with my self-involvement and lack of any concern for others.

My pursuit of a hit album, fame, and recognition was a fast trajectory into one deprecating choice after another. I honestly can't think of a time where I examined my choices and reflected on their effects on myself and those in my life. I was just full steam ahead. This was a direct path to pain. Real pain. Pain for my family. Pain for those who were depending on me. Pain in letting people who trusted me down—and forever losing their trust.

With my lack of attention and interest, my small-town newspaper business began to flounder. Customers were lost. One by one, advertisers and clients ended their patronage. Bills began to pile up and remain unpaid.

Finally, I reached a point where I couldn't ignore what my self-absorption had brought to an end. I was broke and had to sell the business… and hopefully save our home from being repossessed. We had no credit.

Worst of all, I had completely ignored my responsibility as a dad. Another wake-up call came two years after our first child was born. A few weeks after her birth, we received a call from our pediatrician's office to come in for an appointment. Our second child had a difficult delivery. After several weeks that turned into several months, we were concerned with what we were seeing. Our pediatrician reviewed the factors he noted in her development and referred us to a hospital for further testing. She tested behind her age group in most developmental milestones. But no one could predict exactly what that could look like in the years ahead. She would later meet the criteria for a diagnosis of developmentally delayed. One night as I was putting her to bed, the reality suddenly overwhelmed me, and I quietly wept as I watched her sleep.

The newspaper sold to a couple from Boston, and I was able to pay off most of the debts until the buyers suddenly defaulted, and lawsuits ensued for months. I found work at another small weekly newspaper and moved out of the house. Weeks later, I received divorce papers, which I signed without any consultation. I didn't want anything. It could all go—the house, the money, everything. I didn't want any of it.

The gift of the unexpected

Seminary? Seminary!

After my childhood and adolescent experiences with organized religion, I had become quite cynical of anything suggesting religion, God, Jesus, or an after-life in heaven or hell. I saw it as a placebo for weak-minded, highly suggestible people grabbing onto something, anything that gave them assurance in an unpredictable and painful world. Rather, I focused on the ideas of those who disdained such delusions.

But life has a way of rattling one's cage when you least expect it. Something was churning inside of me. I reached the point where one night I was driving alone on a Seattle freeway with no place to go, no one to call, no anything—just me driving to nowhere and nobody.

And then it happened. As I was driving down the freeway, I heard the words that seemed to come from inside me. I heard, "You are loved." I'm not sure how else to describe it. Tears began to pour down my face. Finally, I went to my rental cottage and fell asleep. But I didn't forget what had happened.

While I was in Hawaii months before at an Oahu recording studio completing my next album with a new band, we found ourselves struggling. Our previous rehearsals had all gone well. But now, all of a sudden, we couldn't get a decent take. Over and over again, we tried to just get basic rhythm tracks completed. But our drummer became increasingly intimidated and couldn't even keep a beat. Our producer told us to go back to our hotel and return for a second try after some downtime on the beach.

I couldn't sleep that night. Too much was on the line. I had a tentative offer from a major label, and this was to be my moment for a breakthrough. In the middle of the night, I turned on the TV to stop my brain from continually rolling over the same worries and worst-case scenarios. I stopped clicking the remote channel at a documentary that caught my attention. It was about some 18th-century scientist who experimented with Eastern meditation practices and wrote several books on his experiences and insights. I was intrigued. And since I couldn't sleep anyway, I watched the whole program.

Returning to Seattle a week later, I looked up his name in the public library and found a foundation that published and distributed his writings. The listing included a New York City

The gift of the unexpected

office phone number. I called asking for more information and if there were any contact persons in the Seattle area.

The foundation's office gave me the name and phone number of a Jungian therapist practicing in Seattle. I immediately gave him a call, and we made arrangements to meet the next week.

When I arrived at his Bellevue office, I met a 60-something-year-old man with an Albert Einstein hairdo, wearing a bright Hawaiian shirt and offering a welcoming smile. I shared my story of seeing the middle of the night documentary, which he found quite interesting. He even fielded my questions about himself and his work.

His name was David ... and he would change my life.

He invited me to one of his weekly discussion groups, which I attended the following week. I arrived to find a small group of warm, friendly, interesting people welcoming me. I honestly do not remember what the topic was for the week, but what I *did* remember was what a different atmosphere it was from anything I had ever experienced. There was openness, acceptance, comfort with times of silence or laughter, expressions of gratitude, and most of all; there was kindness.

I asked David if I could meet with him one on one, which he welcomed. At our first meeting, I poured out my questions as he patiently listened. It was my first exposure to ideas of spirituality other than any set religious creed. He spoke of seeing life itself as a spiritual existence, of common human values throughout the world although given different names; of seeing sacred texts speaking of inner spirituality rather than external worldly events.

He would leave me each week with more than enough to contemplate and digest in seven short days. I was at his door like clockwork each week. And he would kindly field my questions and provide me with concepts to consider with each answer.

Then came the monthly potluck and reflection gathering. When everyone sat for the reflection, David was holding a Bible. He read a few scriptures, offered some thoughts, welcomed group members to share their thoughts and feelings, and closed with communion. He indicated all were welcome to participate if they chose to. I was not quite sure how to respond to something directly out of my past that I had thoroughly rejected. But I remained silent. As he read and passed the elements, suddenly, I couldn't stop the tears. The moment had touched on an incredible amount of pain.

As weeks went by, I became a regular at the discussion and reflection groups and continued to have new ideas to contemplate in my weekly one on ones with David. Then, one day, he casually mentioned, "You know, we have a school in Boston.

The president of the school will be visiting in a couple of weeks. Would you like to meet him?"

I immediately expressed interest. The school was a graduate-level seminary offering a Master of Divinity degree in theology, world religions, and pastoral counseling.

I met the visiting president at David and his wife Elizabeth's home. David offered his study for us to meet. I sat across from a man who looked a bit like Colonel Sanders with a white mustache and goatee beard—the president of the school. When he spoke, he spoke with a stutter. I listened as he described the school, campus, and programs and indicated there would be an opening in the fall. Students' housing and a stipend for living expenses would be provided while studying at the school.

I had only completed two years of undergraduate work at my parents' alma mater and wouldn't qualify for acceptance at a graduate school. When I shared this concern, he offered an alternative—I could complete my bachelor's degree at the same time I was going to graduate school as a conditional acceptance to the program.

The very person who had rejected all aspects of religion was now applying to be admitted to a seminary! But this opportunity was like nothing I had ever witnessed before. I was more than curious and wanted to learn about everything the school had to offer. The school president was also a member of the faculty, and would later become my advisor. He, too, would be someone who changed my life. When I began attending his classes listening to his lectures with his slow, difficult stutter, he would continually introduce me to ideas I had never considered before. And after his classes, I would inevitably have to take long walks to just process what he had introduced.

The gift of starting over

From the basement up

When I had met with the president of the school in Seattle, he indicated I would have a small apartment assigned to me. But as I arrived at the campus in late August, the only human being to be found was the caretaker. He had no idea about who I was or where I was supposed to stay. And, to make matters feel more desperate, I was down to my last few dollars. The caretaker made some phone calls and returned to tell me the apartments were all taken, but I could use a basement room that a former student had just moved out of. The "apartment" was a filthy storage room with a sink and a toilet in the hallway.

I was exhausted. I knew no one, had no money and no food with a basement storage room to sleep in. It was the worst possible situation I could have imagined. The caretaker noted there was plenty of food in an upstairs meeting room from a recent committee that had just finished meeting. He helped me move the dusty basement furniture to make some semblance of a living space. After my contacting the president of the school, who was out of town, he authorized my receiving an advance on my monthly stipend. I went directly to the grocery store. So, with the caretaker providing cleaning supplies, the basement storage room became my first Boston home. While school was yet to start, I was given minimum-wage odd jobs by the caretaker to bring in some extra income. I had managed to go from being a successful newspaper publisher to raking leaves and polishing classroom woodwork in a matter of weeks. It was a very, very humbling experience.

Fall semester arrived, and suddenly, the school was buzzing with students, professors, administrators, and committees. To kick things off, the school held an open house for mingling and getting acquainted. The evening event quickly turned into clearly defined small groups. I wandered from group to group, trying to make connections with some minor successes. Suddenly, I heard someone raise their voice, and all attention turned in that direction. On the floor lay our unconscious school president with the crowd around him attempting to do something—anything! After a few minutes of chaos, someone finally got to a phone and called 911. An ambulance arrived, and EMTs placed him on a gurney and rushed him out the door.

Needless to say, the social was over, and the conversations abruptly ended. I turned to one of the professors and asked which hospital the president would be taken to. He had no idea. I escaped to the basement alone, my fear suddenly taking control. I began yelling toward the ceiling screaming at God. "Don't do this! Don't let him die! Don't leave me here alone!"

I was in full-blown, red-alert fear and couldn't stop until I was finally able to breathe and calm myself down. He was my only contact in this strange new place. I didn't know anybody else and was completely dependent on him. I returned upstairs to an almost empty building. The professor I had spoken with gestured toward me and said, "I know which hospital he's at. Do you want to go with me?" I nodded "yes," and we were on our way. We sat in the hospital waiting room for what seemed like endless hours until a nurse came to find us. "He's going to be OK," she said. "We'll keep him overnight for observation."

A few weeks later, on the first day of classes, I was introduced to all my first-year courses and professors and given overviews of materials and expectations. It quickly became clear that I would be doing a great deal of writing. And, miraculously, I would be doing all that writing in an upstairs apartment that had just opened up, thanks to a departing student. I moved my few personal belongings out of the basement, and as I carried my loads up the stairs, I began to get acquainted with my peers. One by one, those peers—who were at different levels of approaching graduation—wandered into my room and introduced themselves. All were very curious about me.

Discovering Unexpected Gifts

I quickly learned that the group's norm was evening ad hoc debates on theology, philosophy, eschatology, ontology, epistemology, and every other "ology" one could think of. This wasn't a competition about physical strength or how much alcohol one could handle or whose sports team was best. It was all about evaluating different philosophical concepts and carefully dissecting those constructed theories and ideologies. This was their entertainment!

They were brilliant. And I was out of my league. However, two of the students were beginning guitar players. With their learning of my background, a "music room" was quickly created in the basement storage room with discarded carpet serving as sound muting on the walls—just under the school president's office. As soon as classes ended and the school began to empty, we would head to the music room to attempt replicating our favorite musicians and songs. I learned later that our school president could hear it all and patiently put up with our noise without saying a word. In fact, he joked that we should add to the school's application, "What instrument do you play?"

The gift of belonging

Student poor, constantly studying, writing papers, holding down a part-time job and loving it

It didn't take long for my routine to settle in. I was either in class, thinking about class, or writing something for class. I grew to increasingly appreciate my professors and their idiosyncrasies. It was clear they enjoyed their whipping us into intellectual shape, bit by bit. After being out of school for a decade, this was a steep learning curve for me. But I relished everything I was learning. Some of the students complained of our school president's stutter, but I found that no problem at all. He would later tell me that when he had to give a speech, his speech coach would have him practice by singing the words.

Although I had left the assets of our weekly newspaper sale (and our home) in the divorce, I needed to pay child support. That meant finding a job I could fit in between the hours of study and classes. My solution came with taking a direct-care staff position at a group home for adult developmentally delayed men who also struggled with mental illness. I quickly learned that the position was like a revolving door, as many staff came and went as quickly as they came. But with my own daughter diagnosed with what would later be called a cognitive impairment, I wanted to learn more about what her care would require as she grew up.

It was a challenging job. The four residents were aggressive and could be dangerous. If Scott became frustrated, he was capable of pulling the bathroom sink off the wall and throwing it. Fred could leap from the stairs and attack from behind if angry or frustrated by not getting what he wanted. Eddie often had the mildest behavior, just constantly rocking on the sofa, but could unexpectedly slap you across the head. John was shy and timid and yet could suddenly go into a rage of unknown perceived threats and put his fist through a window.

Then I met Neil. Neil had been working at the home for years. He was instantly in charge when he arrived for the day and would kindly greet and check on each of the residents as he went through the house. They all knew he cared. And they all knew he was in charge. Neil was an advocate and insisted that the men he cared for had the same privilege and rights as any other adult. Neil would teach them basic life skills by bringing everyone to the bank and the grocery store. He would reward new accomplishments, such as using an ATM or assisting in cooking a meal with praise and appreciation. And Neil had no patience for any staff who thought the job was sitting on the sofa watching TV. Staff who arrived looking for an easy job soon found themselves being shown the door.

Neil and I quickly became friends, and as a team, we began converting the house into a home with attention to detail and organization. Nothing broken remained in the house. Residents joined in working side by side with Neil, helping him make improvements. The house's whole energy changed when he arrived.

Soon, we were taking community outings with the company van. Neil always insisted that the residents we cared for have every opportunity for mainstreaming in the community. We went to my school campus to play basketball on the outdoor court. We went to walk through the mall and to visit the ice cream store. Doctor and dentist appointments were carefully kept.

My workplace became my second home. All of us, including me, felt like we belonged. And I grew to feel the same at school. I was where I needed to be, and where I *belonged*.

The gift of "yes"

Living in two worlds

The time soon came for my requirement of completing my bachelor's degree. I had spoken with my advisor about my core passion for writing music and my interest in coordinating with other disciplines such as live theatre or film. I asked about the possibility of introducing media to the school's visibility and outreach. He urged me to consider applying to Emerson College in downtown Boston with a performing arts and communications specialist focus.

I contacted the theatre arts admissions director, Paul Brown, and made an appointment. As I shared my past composing and recording projects with him, including creating a multimedia performance project using live music, actors, film, and special effects, he reviewed my portfolio of storyboards and albums. I also disclosed my situation with conditional acceptance at my graduate school.

Paul listened with interest and indicated his seeing my participation at Emerson as a good fit with the theatre department's programs. He expressed concern about scheduling classes but left that to my responsibility. I thanked him for his considering me for admission and left with my fingers crossed. I would also be a non-traditional student in my early 30s, which made me even more of an exception.

As I was completing my first summer clinical experience assignment in Seattle, I received a packet in the mail. It was from Emerson College admissions. Not only was I accepted, but I was provided with a full financial aid award with scholarships, grants, and loans. When I returned to Boston in the fall, I went directly to the theatre arts office to express my thanks to Paul. I was stunned when I was informed that he had passed away. He had made a huge impact on my life with his saying "yes" to my application, and I would never be able to express my gratitude to him face to face.

Suddenly, my life became amazingly full, with morning classes at graduate school and afternoon/evening classes at Emerson. I was learning everything I could about every aspect of theatre, film, and video production. My curriculum included writing classes, directing, set design, lighting, video studio production, and acting. Soon, professors and students began approaching me for composing music for their productions. I was in creative heaven! My Emerson professors would tease me that I would learn more about performing behind the pulpit from them than I had from my seminary.

Though I never got to tell him in person, the gift of Paul Brown's supporting my creative development and expression will never be forgotten.

The gift of presence

A home visit

My summer clinical experiences were a chance to set aside the books, exams, and term papers. Life shifted to a hands-on, in-person summer of spending time with a supervisor, students from other schools, and, most importantly, with patients and their families. Choices ran the gamut from hospitals to institutions. To be able to enjoy summers with my two children, I chose sites that were either close to their home or where I could bring them with me. My first choice was a Seattle facility named Fircrest School. Fircrest was envisioned as being a center for the support, care, and skill-building of adult men and women diagnosed with severe or profound mental retardation (the term used at that time). It was an entire gated campus with medical staff, therapists, caregivers, recreational and vocational facilitators with residents living in a series of dormitories based on diagnostic needs.

My unit for the summer included Cherry Hall—a unit for immobilized, non-verbal men and women requiring 24/7 intensive care. Our daily internship routine included morning silence in the chapel for one hour, discussion on a specific topic in the morning staff meeting, one on ones with our supervisor, and providing a chapel service for residents. We were also expected to be present in our units throughout the day and develop relationships with caregiving staff.

I was honestly quite intimidated with my start at Fircrest. I didn't know what to do or what to say, or even how to be helpful. Ironically, as the summer transpired, I found my attitude completely reversed, with my feeling most at ease with my days on campus before returning to "the outside world" of pretense and indifference. None of that existed within the walls of Fircrest. When I first introduced myself to the staff, I found a common thread. Most had taken a position they thought would be temporary, only to find themselves still there many years later. There was something indescribable about the peaceful atmosphere in the midst of such vulnerability that touched everyone. One of my clients named Fred had come to Fircrest following a skyscraper construction site accident where he was struck by a swinging structural beam, causing permanent prefrontal cortex brain damage. I would take Fred on walks in his wheelchair, and the whole time he would be waving his arms, trying to grab at me while he roared. Over time, that diminished. But what gave him the most calming moments was when I read the sports pages to him each day.

My supervisor, Bill, encouraged me to contact family members of my clients. Calling complete strangers to invite myself to visit them seemed even more intimidating than my initial working at the campus with residents. Who was I to interfere with their personal lives? My supervisor told me to start with Fred's family. I made the call to his home and introduced myself to his mother. I was apologetic about bothering her, only to hear her express she would be glad to see me. When I arrived at her home, she welcomed me in and offered refreshments. When I asked about what had happened to Fred, she shared his story in a soft-spoken voice. I thanked her for sharing with me.

I thought I was about ready to leave, but she wanted to show me family photos on the wall. One by one, we went from photo to photo of fond memories. But then we came to her deceased husband's photo. She found a chair and sat down, and invited me to do the same.

"Do you know what he said to me just before he died?" she asked.

I gestured with a "No," and she began to weep.

"He told me to go to hell."

I sat silently with her, trying to think of something comforting to say. I ended up saying nothing. But somehow, I had earned her trust. She stood and thanked me profusely for coming to see her. I assured her I would continue to check in on Fred.

I left feeling so inadequate. But when I shared my experience with my supervisor later, he just nodded and said, "You did the right thing."

The lesson given to all of us interns was about presence. Just being present. I couldn't see the point or the value of that. When I visited my unit, I wanted to help *do* things—help with feeding, help with taking clients on walks in their wheelchairs. But time and time again, Bill would pull me back and repeat, "Just be present."

In time, it began to sink in. Staff felt comfortable around me and enjoyed my being there. Often, I would be told their favorite stories or why they chose their work. I was a member of the team; the community.

Sunday chapels were unique to Fircrest. Residents would be wheeled to the chapel and lined up. It was a noisy time together as voices rose and softened. Bill would use a picture book and tell a Bible story, and we would sing Sunday school songs, offering peace to each participant and help returning everyone to their unit.

Part of our clinical experience included weekly one on one sessions with Bill. He had a way of just looking right through you. I would sit silently across from him in his small office, and he would remain silent as well. The minutes would tick away, our hour would come to an end, and I would be dismissed. The next week would be a repeat of the week before and continue week after week.

Then, one day, Bill broke the silence. "You know this is *your* time, don't you? You can do with it what you want. It's not my time. It's yours."

I looked at him for a moment, and suddenly, the words just spilled out after years and years of being denied friendships, living in isolation, incompetent at what it was like to have caring relationships.

"I feel so alone." The tears quickly followed. After I gathered myself, Bill quietly spoke. "You know, you and Fred are a lot alike." I wasn't sure where he was going.

"Fred doesn't have anybody. He doesn't have anyone come to see him. Doesn't have any family. You and he have a lot in common. Kind of like brothers."

I sat silent for a moment. I got his point. But the most amazing thing was the instant lightness I felt when I said those words after holding them for so long. I realized that letting someone else in, letting someone else hold the pain or hurt or loss with you takes away its power. I had a whole new attitude about what presence meant—Bill had just given me the gift of his presence.

Fircrest no longer exists. Policies changed to mainstreaming residents with staffed apartments, assisted transportation, and daily routines of living in the community. But for me, I would say I learned more in that one summer than all the "brilliant" theological term papers I ever completed. They're stuck in a filing cabinet somewhere. But what's stuck in me is what I learned at Fircrest.

It's really all about presence.

The gift of suddenly having your world shaken

My seven-year-old introduction to racism

The last week of my clinical experience came with the news that my grandfather had died. I didn't really have any sort of reaction. My mom told me she was flying to Texas for the funeral and asked if I wanted to go. As I said, "No," I was somewhat puzzled at my lack of any emotion. I had no good memories of my grandfather. Actually, the ones I had were far from cherished—it was more like wishing I didn't have any at all. I felt no sadness, no grief, just nothing. The last time I saw him in my early 20s, he had come to Washington State to vacation and see my mom. He would pull stunts like traveling across the country with his Cadillac pulling his Airstream trailer using only silver dollars to pay for everything, fully enjoying the shock value from everyone's reactions. After his visit came to an end and he was saying his goodbyes, he walked up to me, shook my hand, and softly said, "You'll never amount to a pile of shit, kid." That was my last memory of the guy.

Every other summer, my parents would make the *long* drive from Washington State to Beaumont, Texas, to spend weeks with my mom's family. At the time, I had no clue how much my dad hated the obligation, but there was no denying the fact that he was the one who had taken Mom so far from the family.

For me, the trip was a voyage of endless boredom sitting in the back seat alone. I would entertain myself by reading the Burma Shave signs with only a few words posted every few miles, eventually making a complete sales message. And then there were the "so many miles to Stuckey's" countdown signs. Stopping was an absolute treat.

I was too young to pick up on the charged energy between my dad and grandfather. I would only learn of that later. For me, it was hanging out with my cousin David who was constantly barefoot and didn't wince a bit when he stepped on the sharp gravel road rocks. And then there were my older four girl cousins who listened to the Archies and teased me about daring to kiss them. The community pool was a daily routine, and my cousin David thought nothing of jumping off the high dive forward, backward, any which way. I stuck with the low dive.

My mom and grandmother would visit for hours in the kitchen, and after the evening meal, my grandparents would get out their two electric guitars and play and sing their favorite country songs.

I was given permission to walk from the house to my grandfather's small gas station/food store and get one free soda each day. I would watch my grandpa sitting in a rocker with his peers, passing the time, making jokes, and complaining about the heat.

One day, as I was sipping my soda just outside the station, I saw an older pickup truck pull up to the gas pump. In the back were three kids—one looked about my age. My initial reaction was joy, thinking I had somebody I could play with.

But then the most confusing, unexpected thing happened. My grandfather came running out of the store, screaming, "Get out of my gas station, n_____" I glanced at the faces of the kids in the back and then to the man and woman in the cab and made note of the fear in their eyes. My grandfather repeated his words, and I watched as they started their truck and pulled away.

I had no idea what to think. I had never seen my grandfather act like that before. What did these people do to make him so mad? I can still see their faces. In fact, they are permanently placed in my consciousness.

I don't remember talking to any of my family about the incident. I wasn't sure what to ask or who I could go to. But I wanted to understand what had happened.

Two years later, on the next expedition to Texas, I would learn much more. My grandfather left church with all of us in his Cadillac and stopped at a restaurant for Sunday dinner. He told us to stay in the car, then marched into the diner to tell every person of color to get out before he would allow us to come in. I was old enough at that point to know real shame. I had no power, but I did have resolve that I would never be like my grandfather.

The world continued to open my eyes and challenge my ignorance. In second grade, as the class exchanged Christmas presents, I watched my friend Eddy crying at his desk. "Why is Eddy crying?" I asked my teacher.

"Eddy is Jewish," she replied. "He doesn't celebrate Christmas."

I was suddenly becoming aware of privilege—*my* privilege—and I was equally becoming aware that this did not feel right. I didn't understand why we would treat people differently. And the confusion rolled around and around in me, shaping my inability to accept my first shock at the world I had never seen before.

It has shaped me ever since.

The gift of closed doors

Not what I had planned

A couple sayings come to mind as I approached graduation from both Emerson and seminary. The first is, "When one door closes, another door will open ... but the hallway is hell."

The other is, "Living is what we do while we're busy making other plans." Or, put another way, "I'm grateful most of my plans didn't work out."

As I drew closer to losing the security of student life, I became increasingly anxious. Where was I going to find a job? How would I survive? What do you do with degrees in theatre arts and theology?

I began receiving invitations from various parishes to candidate at their churches. St Louis, Minneapolis, Detroit, Cincinnati, a retreat center/summer camp in Michigan—I visited them all. My hopes of work writing music for movie/television production studios came to a dead end when I realized that getting into the business required a year of full-time internship with no pay. There was no way I could do that. Other theatre student peers had family resources to take internships. That was simply not an option for me.

I found each parish I visited to be mostly small communities of elderly parishioners. And, uniformly, they had no interest in growth or change but rather wanted to continue with the same comforting traditions and routines they cherished.

My one opportunity of interest was the retreat center/summer camp—mostly a year-round operation with caregivers overseeing the property. The place bustled with families and kids during the summer and had steady groups throughout the fall and winter for different interests and focuses. The largest was an annual teen winter break retreat with kids coming from around the region to the tune of 50 to 70 participants.

I also learned of a pastoral care position opening serving the emergency center and pediatric intensive care unit at Beaumont Hospital in the Detroit area. The hospital was huge, with 900 beds and 80,000 admissions a year.

Both sounded like opportunities I would welcome. And both accepted my applications. I was moving to Detroit. In a whirlwind of activity, I finalized my new positions, wrapped up my school obligations, packed my things, and sat with my cap and gown on the stage of a college auditorium. Five years ago, I couldn't have imagined I would end up becoming an ordained minister—not even in my wildest dreams. I was different now. I could feel it in the shift from an angry, self-absorbed, "got all the answers" mindset to one of humility, wanting to make a difference, and absolutely no clue what would come next.

The gift of witnessing our humanity

A few hours together

After filling out countless forms and completing orientations, I was officially a member of the pastoral care team at Beaumont Hospital. I worked with peers from several different denominations and traditions, but we each had individual schedules and areas, leaving us mostly working alone. My shifts were nights, from 11 p.m. to 7 a.m., with the emergency center and pediatric intensive care. I was expected to be focused on family members as their loved one was being treated.

It didn't take long to become accustomed to the sights, sounds, and smells of the "green room," where emergency surgeries and interventions occurred at a rapid pace. The patient waiting rooms and areas were filled every night, and a good part of my time was spent with each person, offering my support. I was paged when the ER staff needed me to be present with waiting family members as they would receive news about their loved one. My years at Beaumont Hospital would leave me with countless memories of those who would look to me for comfort and support in the few hours we would spend together.

Providing pastoral care can be unique in that you are with family members through extremely intense events, emotions, and often grief for just a few hours—then you never see them again. When I received a page from intensive care or pediatric intensive care in the middle of the night, I had an idea of what to expect. But each person I met, each family I sat with, left a unique, precious impression on me. I was given permission to witness; to be present in perhaps the most difficult, most painful moments of their lives. And I was privileged to witness their strength, kindness, vulnerability, sorrow, and commitment to caring for one another.

Many times, my presence was simply sitting quietly with a family member. I'll never forget:

- The mother whose high school-aged son came home complaining of a headache, only to hours later collapse from an aneurism. We sat together by his bed most of the night. The next morning, she asked to authorize donating his organs to help others.

- The foster mom who received medically fragile children from social services. I was paged to be with her as she sat with a foster child who was the victim of shaken baby syndrome. Her name was Kelly. And during the night,

Kelly died. I found myself unable to hold back the tears as I sat with this caring foster mom. Later, I would share in my supervision with the pastoral care director that I wasn't there for that foster mom, being caught in my own grief. He affirmed that sometimes weeping together is precisely the care we provide.

A few days later, I made contact with the foster mom, asking if I could visit her. She welcomed the request. I arrived at a modest home that looked like a full-blown hospital unit on the inside. Every room seemed to be filled with medical equipment as I met the children she cared for. "What brought you to becoming a foster mom for these children?" I asked.

She just smiled and replied, "Somebody's gotta do it. It might as well be me."

I had made a wonderful new friend that I would see from time to time in the hospital's pediatric unit.

- The tiny, soft-spoken, elderly mom who was sitting next to her adult son's intensive care bed. She shared with me this was her only living son, a doctor, after losing her two other sons.

As we sat together, she quietly said to me, "I'm mad at God," and then returned to her silence. During the night, her son died as efforts to resuscitate him failed. It was almost morning when she was ready to leave. She looked at me and asked, "Will God forgive me if I don't go to church Sunday?" She was serious. I just held her hands in mine for a while, and then she was on her way.

- The parents who lost their stillborn child. I was paged by one of the nurses and found her in the nurses' station. "It would mean a lot to them if you would baptize the baby," she told me. I would not have the opportunity to meet them, but the nurse brought me to where the baby was laid and left me alone. For a while, I was caught in a dilemma of conflicting values and beliefs in making a decision. But, for some reason, in that moment, none of that mattered. I provided the ritual baptism for the child and returned to inform the nurse.

- The 19-year-old mom next to her baby who was resting in an incubator alone in the darkened pediatric intensive care room. I listened as she told her story of her and her younger brother being taken from their mother, raised by various indifferent relatives who passed them around, escaping to end up living on the streets. She shared that she wanted to have a baby just to have someone to love and who loved her.

- The grandmother who asked to have a chaplain paged so she could talk with someone before going into surgery the next morning. As I introduced myself, she burst into tears. "I don't know what's wrong with me. I've been a faithful Christian all my life. And I try to live my faith to the best of my ability every day. But I'm scared. I am failing in my trust in God." We talked through the night of the Bible stories she knew of those who were afraid as they faced their callings, including Christ as he faced crucifixion. I could see she was both relaxing more, growing tired, and I left with a prayer. When I checked in on her the next day, I found her doing just fine.

My work would also include checking in with staff in the break room and listening to the challenges they had faced that night. At 7 a.m., we would all slowly walk to the staff parking lot—quiet and exhausted, returning to our own lives for a few hours after a morning sleep.

The routine would begin the next evening, and the next, and so on. In my years at Beaumont, I would be introduced to an incredible number of inspiring people of different faiths, traditions, ages, and cultures. What they taught me remains with me. I had been given permission and welcomed to be a witness in their lives.

The gift of supporting each other

Summer camp and teen retreats

My second job living in the Detroit area involved something quite different than hospital pastoral care. I would describe it as something like controlled chaos—with more emphasis on the *chaos* part. Each summer and each winter break, I would take leave from my white hospital chaplain's jacket and shift to hoodies, jeans, and, of course, the camp's official T-shirt.

Both the summer camp and teen retreats were exercises in learning to function without enough sleep. The rural Michigan camp had been around for generations, with the black and white photos on dorm and kitchen walls to prove it. And with the history came traditions—lots of traditions. If you wanted to become one of the most unpopular camp directors ever, you just had to suggest trying a new or ending an old tradition.

Weeks before anyone arrived for a camp or a retreat event, I was busy planning meetings, completing state health and department documents, training staff, meeting inspectors, and getting out the publicity materials.

Camp was a lockstep routine of getting to breakfast, cleaning your dorm, arriving at the flagpole, going to the chapel for morning events, lunch, rest hour (for the adults), afternoon activities, swimming in the lake, showers, dinner, and some evening-themed activity such as carnival night or camp Olympics. But the most important part of the day was always seeing the candy lady after lunch with your allotted allowance for some exceedingly difficult candy decisions.

The teen retreat held each winter break also had its structure, but it was much more about free time and hanging out with friends you hadn't seen since the previous year's winter retreat.

I found my niche in both by borrowing from skills learned at Emerson. During the summer afternoons, teens would prepare a play for a final Saturday night performance in the rec hall. I would assist the teens with brainstorming ideas, creating, and rehearsing topics important to them, and each year, there would be a brand new premiere ready to present to the camp. Every teen was involved either on or behind the stage. The teens identified themselves as SAG—the Survivor's Acting Guild. Without anyone really noticing, I had created the unheard-of new tradition!

For winter retreat, I would bring over adult staff who enjoyed connecting with teens to create a mixture of play, hanging out, lots of food and snacks, and serious discussion time on topics affecting them. Year after year, we would see teens show up from all over the country, inviting their friends and staying connected with each other until the next winter retreat.

Adult staff played dual roles in keeping behavioral boundaries and having fun with the kids. Often, I would hear from teens how important the retreat was to them. My teenage son wouldn't miss it even though his dad was there (whom he completely ignored the entire week.) Many of the teens came from not-so-great home environments or rejection and harassment at school. One of those kids was named Kyle (not his real name). Kyle and my son became close friends, enjoying getting into as much mischief as they could. But, as each winter retreat came to an end, they knew they would have to wait to see each other again at summer camp.

And then the phone call came that changed everything. It was the campground caretaker. He had found Kyle outside the dormitory on the ground. He had shot himself. Inside his car, the police found a note left behind saying that the camp was the only place he had felt loved.

I was in absolute shock. I knew immediately I had to be the one to tell my son. Word spread quickly among all the teens who participated in winter retreat, and just as quickly came calls for getting together to share the loss together and care for one another.

A date was set, and all were notified. I arrived a day early to get things ready, and as I walked into the kitchen, I saw our camp cook preparing food for the arrivals. I went to her to give her a hug, and suddenly I found myself weeping on her shoulder. She just held me for a while. I was grateful to her for not only holding me and allowing me to let my pain out, but for my being able to be there for all who would arrive later.

This was a life-changing moment for all of us. As we shared and listened and made commitments for caring for each other, the group (including parents attending) grew incredibly close. My son and I often talked about Kyle over the years. It was an OK topic to bring up at any time. Sometimes we brought it up to laugh at the silly things he and my son did. Other times it was to ponder "Why?" one more time.

Most of those teens, now adults, remain in close contact. And they have now become the leaders of that summer camp/retreat center. They also have made some new traditions of their own to add to the precious ones that came before them.

The gift of powerlessness

When the injuries cannot heal, when the damage can't be undone, but you still show up

After serving at Beaumont Hospital and the camp/retreat center for seven years, I was offered an opportunity to return to Washington State with a position at a spiritual growth center leading community programs. I saw this as an opportunity to be closer to my children and spend more time with them. Ironically, however, my son received a full scholarship to an Ohio University and would leave just months after my return. Over the years, we had found ways to be close: phone calls and letters and summers together. I was thrilled for the opportunity for him but found myself sad I would still be a long-distance dad. Now, it was *his* turn to leave for school.

The spiritual growth center turned out not to be a fit for me, and my time there ended sooner than was planned. However, another door opened. My years of work with teens and children became a plus for me when I was told of openings at the Seattle YMCA Youth and Family Services program—just in its infancy. The Y had made a commitment just a few years earlier to focus on children in foster care and homeless youth in the Seattle-King County area. My application led to an interview, which led to a job offer. A position as a child and family therapist was open. I would have to complete Washington State accreditation and was given a grace period to prepare for and pass the exam. My weekends became study marathons as I reviewed and read all the suggested materials for preparation. Six months later, a full day of silently checking boxes and writing responses with a room full of other hushed applicants resulted in my passing the exam.

However, passing an exam was a far cry from the experiences I had yet to learn from. I was given my first caseload from the retiring therapist before me. One by one, I went to foster home after foster home to introduce myself. I can't honestly say I was welcomed with open arms. I would describe it more as a "Well, get to work! Look at what we're dealing with. We need help—*now*." And I quickly learned they were telling the truth.

A child who has been in foster care is affected on all levels—cognitively, emotionally, physically, and relationally. Developmentally, one of our first tasks is to determine whether the world is safe or not.

Safe: A child can learn trust, feel empowered to explore, and develop relationships.

The gift of powerlessness

Unsafe: There is fear, anger, rage, and continued victimization played out by the child or adolescent who sees this as normal. This is a child on 24/7 "red alert," unable to focus and learn, and unable to trust.

Foster parents were given twice monthly trainings, peer support meetings, and 24-hour pager support when foster kids in their home acted out with property damage, going on the run, threats with improvised weapons, or putting the parents' own children at risk. The state would provide the Y and foster parents with increased financial support to work with these challenges.

I began my work by developing relationships. By listening. By one on ones. Whenever I found an interest of any kind by a youth in my care, we would pursue it. I began playing a lot of basketball, and I got pretty good at it. But a win with one of my kids on the basketball court was a rare event. And that worked for me.

This also became a time of learning that despite all your progress in working with a child, it could all blow up in an instant. I would get the call from my foster parent. Or the police. Or both.

I noted a fairly steady rate of turnover in our program. But over the months and years, a core group of counselors, case aides, foster parents, and therapists remained who just continued to hang in there. A sense of humor helped. And a common belief of not giving up on a kid who, through no fault of their own, had become so difficult they just really needed somebody who wouldn't give up on them.

Being allowed to be a part of these kids' lives offered many gifts I hadn't anticipated at all. Sometimes the gifts were learning humility. Sometimes the gifts were learning patience. But the most powerful gift was learning and accepting powerlessness—to acknowledge that every loss can't be reconciled, every failure can't have meaning, to try harder doesn't change everything, and to admit I often imposed *my* ideas of what this child or adolescent should do or should be. Sitting with the acknowledgment of powerlessness is POWERFUL. It doesn't mean I give up. It means I wholly give myself to the well-being of a child or youth, even though it might not make a difference at all—to show up without investment in the outcome. The outcome is about me, not the child. Giving fully without expectations is about the child.

The children

A Few of Their Precious Stories
That Remain With Me…

I have changed the following names to anonymously share the gifts each of these children and adolescents left with me. There are many more I could share. But, in considering the ways we as human beings can set our courses in life from the experiences of our childhoods, these innocent ones are examples of amazing strength and courage. I was graced with the privilege of knowing them and receiving their unexpected gifts.

Dave

Dave was an exception. When I met him for the first time, and he introduced himself, he said, "Hi, I'm Dave; I don't have any feelings." Dave had multiple sexual assault charges with younger youth. He required foster parents trained specifically in working with keeping him and other youth safe.

One day, Dave's mother arrived at my office. She stated that she was clean, sober, had her life back together, and would do whatever it took to get her child back. She meant it. And after a long series of court reviews and safety plans, Dave returned to her care. I would continue to see him weekly and was struck by the almost immediate positive changes I saw in him. Years later, I was invited to his high school graduation. It was a proud moment for all of us. Later he would let me know he had enlisted in the Marines.

Mark

Mark also placed all his behaviors on his not being able to be with his mom. His behaviors were so severe he required a lockdown home with constant supervision by staff. With a great deal of searching, Mark's mom was located, and I began facilitating visits at her apartment. A conditional return home was granted, but this time, everything went south. Mark continued his aggressive behaviors in his mom's care. She couldn't handle him, and Mark grew more and more enraged. Police were called, and Mark was arrested for assault. He would return to juvenile justice overseeing, and when he was released, disappeared.

Sam

Sam liked to steal cars. And he was good at it—until he got caught. He was placed with a foster parent diagnosed with CP, or cerebral palsy. This foster parent was barely able to manage living on his own with help from family and friends. Yet, he would take some of the toughest kids into his home. As I would visit each of my youth living with him, I would witness time and time again where kids would become attached to him. They would help out with the things he could no longer do. And you could see the pride in their eyes as they cared for him. Sam remained in the home until the day he got caught trying to steal another car and was sent away to an adolescent lockdown facility located at a remote location. At one point, San ended up in solitary confinement due to his behaviors. I would visit him monthly until his release. Sam contacted me years later to let me know he was OK and going to community college.

Annie

Annie had been continually and severely sexually abused as a child by her mom's "boyfriends." When social services removed her from her mother's apartment into foster care, Annie could always find a way to go on the run. She would repeatedly place herself at risk meeting men in downtown Seattle. Despite best efforts to keep her safe, Annie disappeared. Years later, I would be told she had stopped by the YMCA to see me long after I had left the agency. I was glad to hear she was alive.

Charlie

Charlie suffered from severe PTSD. As a young child, he was living with his parents in a hotel room, which was filled with weapons, explosives, and drugs. The report from the state indicated that a SWAT team made a sudden charge into the hotel room, Charlie was picked up and taken by a social worker, and he never saw his parents again. As a teen, Charlie constantly remained on red alert. He could not hold his hands steady. If a teacher asked him to redo a math problem, odds were good he would go ballistic. Charlie began to calm as time went on with the help of med management and living with a kind and understanding foster mom. She would team up with the school, setting up interventions for Charlie to support him when he felt at risk. He had a "safe place" to go if he needed to calm himself. He was allowed to walk off his stress energy on the school track without question. Yet, I would still receive calls regularly from the school to "come get Charlie."

Logan

Logan was brought into care as he came to social services' attention from a school teacher's 911 call. He was living alone with his mother, who was later diagnosed with schizophrenia. He was essentially caring not only for himself, but for her as well. Logan clearly loved his mother very much, and most of our time was spent making trips to visit with her. He would bring her supplies offered by his foster parents, check on her medicine and other needs, do some cleaning in the apartment, and just sit with her. Logan had become the parent. The weekly visits were extremely important to Logan, making them our routine as we spent time together. He lived with a single foster dad who had recently lost his wife to cancer. The two of them bonded like dorm buddies, with Logan taking full responsibility for getting his schoolwork done and caring for himself. Logan later moved to another foster home where he received much-needed nurturing and care. As a high school graduate, he opted for community college with an interest in majoring in computer science. I kept in touch with Logan from time to time and learned he had gotten his driver's license and his first car. He used that car to visit and care for his mother.

Luke

Luke was rescued from an extremely violent home situation. He was clearly traumatized and often would put himself at risk to somehow feel normal. Luke was emotionally sensitive and found he felt more comfortable wearing women's clothes and makeup. He was also an easy target for bullies, and sadly was often harassed or even beaten. His single foster dad became Luke's advocate with no uncertain terms. If something happened to Luke at school, his foster dad was in the office. Somebody harassed his foster son, he insisted on a meeting with all his teachers. Luke also needed constant monitoring with his behaviors as he was highly sexualized and suggestible. Luke's foster dad and I became good friends as we worked together to advocate for him. His happiest moments were preparing for Halloween, where he could freely dress up in women's clothes and parade around his foster home.

But Luke eventually aged out of foster care and suddenly was on his own. Attempts to qualify him for Social Security or other benefits failed as he was found to have "too high of an IQ score."

I received a call from the foster dad a few weeks later. Luke was in the King County Jail for indecent behavior in a public bathroom. We both visited him but with his release soon lost touch. He never reappeared.

Gary

Gary had a history perhaps most of us would not have survived. He was left at a Romanian orphanage by his Roma, or gypsy parents. Roma was a term used to slur his heritage, and would be considered the lowest class in his country. The orphanage was essentially a baby warehouse. The understaffed and underfunded facility was room after room of small cribs with babies changed and fed by too few caregivers. That was it. No interaction. No stimulation or affection. Just survival.

A Seattle couple flew to Romania and adopted Gary through their church's adoption program as he turned three years old. When he arrived at his new home, he asked his adoptive parents when they would be leaving. He assumed they were staff like those he had known for the first three years of his life. Gary was severely developmentally late on all his milestones, and soon showed signs of aggression toward his adoptive parents and their daughters. At one point, he attempted to use a knife as a weapon.

The couple essentially gave up on Gary and notified social services of their not being able to care for him. Gary was placed in a group care facility with peer-age children. It was there that I had my first chance to meet him. I introduced myself and told him about foster care at the YMCA. And then we played some basketball at the facilities' outdoor court.

Gary went through the process of becoming a foster child with great difficulty. He quickly gained a reputation for being aggressive and angry. One by one, Gary blew out of the foster homes he was placed in. That is, until one day, when he met Bob.

Bob had recently lost his wife suddenly to aggressive cancer. And after starting life over without her, he decided he would continue fostering children by himself and brought Gary into his home.

He had already heard all the stories at the foster parent meetings. Gary did his usual array of, "Get me out of here" behaviors. But Bob would just respond, "That the best you got?" Bob held Gary accountable on all fronts. At home, in the community, and at school. Bob was at Gary's school almost daily. But somehow, it finally sunk in with Gary that he wasn't going to be able to get kicked out of this home, and he finally relaxed. He began getting good grades at school. He signed up for the school play and took a small part (that he was very proud of). And you couldn't have seen a prouder foster dad and son on Gary's graduation day.

Gary got help from different agencies and scholarships and completed community college, got accepted to the University of Washington, and completed his master's at the University of Chicago. He is now a mental health therapist for youth and families in Washington State. Gary keeps in touch with his foster dad and with me. It makes my day every time I hear from him.

Carla

Carla was one of the most violent and pervasive self-harming youth I had ever met. She was referred to the Y's most intensive foster care program following an incident where she took a light bulb from a group care facility, crushed it, and swallowed the pieces of broken glass. Carla was one very, very angry teenage girl.

One of the Y's foster moms asked for Carla as soon as she was admitted to their foster care program. This foster mom had seen it all and had a reputation for sticking with kids regardless of what they tried to pull on her. Carla tried everything she could think of to get kicked out of the home, but nothing worked. This foster mom was also an ordained minister with a small congregation in Seattle. That meant Carla had a choice of staying at a respite foster parent's on Sunday or going to church. After a few respite tries, Carla decided to try going to a Sunday service.

Carla experienced unconditional love. She had never had that before. Much of Carla's anger drew from the rejection she repeatedly experienced from her bio mom and dad, who were divorced and living separately. Carla would keep going back to each of them, only to be turned away. It was later learned that her bio dad had sexually abused her as a child.

Carla got into lots of trouble as her anger drove her actions and behaviors. But her foster mom would dust her off, have a long talk with her, give some consequences, and start over again. Carla found someone who accepted her no matter what. She stopped going to her parents' homes seeking the affection which would never come. She started doing well in school. And her self-esteem grew week by week in the nurturing home she could trust in. Years later, after Carla had moved on from foster care to her own independent life, she came to visit me at my YMCA office.

We found a private place to talk. She shared of her successes in college and her career hopes. And then she said something that made me smile. "You know Steve," she said, "my parents are assholes." I didn't say a thing but just gave her a big smile. She knew I totally got what she was telling me.

* * *

These children, these teens, gave me many more gifts than I believe I gave them. They opened my eyes as they shared their pain. They taught me how fragile we really are without the absolutely essential nurturing every human being needs. They showed me amazing resilience I thought I would never see. They taught me how to be a counselor, a witness, and how to give and receive unconditionally.

The gift of unconditional love

Elizabeth

Earlier I wrote of my attending a community gathering at Dave Johnson's office. It was there that I met his wife, Elizabeth. I immediately found her to be warm, gracious, and open. Following my move to Boston to start school, I kept in touch with both Dave and Elizabeth. And, when returning to Seattle, I would always visit them in their home. Both had such a kind way of being and thoroughly loved a good laugh. When I returned to Seattle to begin work at the YMCA, I would make a habit of visiting them regularly and often had one on one coffee with David to talk therapy, philosophy, theology, current events, or whatever captured our interest. David and Elizabeth were in their late 60s when I first met them, and they came to be a regular part of my life in the years that followed. David was about to turn 100 when he died. Elizabeth deeply grieved his loss. I began checking in more often for short visits with her as her energy diminished. Her daughter came to live with her and provide for Elizabeth being able to remain in her home.

I can't fully describe Elizabeth's presence. But if I were to pick a word, it would be kindness. She loved reading the latest books on spirituality and universal connections being made by the world's religions. She was very much an optimist and a believer that the world will become a better place as we evolve as a people. I would sit with her and just listen, enjoying every moment. Even though she had five adult children and many grandchildren and great-grandchildren, she always had time for me. She was the first person who ever told me, "I am proud of you."

Elizabeth had watched me stumble and fall many times over the years in my choices and relationships. But never did I hear a word of criticism or disapproval. She would listen. And she would share her own life experiences and how they had affected and shaped her. She was my best friend, and she was an artist—both literally *and* as a way of being.

However, her body began to fail her, and suddenly, the focus became keeping her comfortable and closely monitored as hospice care was provided at her home. Her children, grandchildren, and great-grandchildren from all parts of the country gathered to be near her. She had just turned 100.

The day came when I received a call from one of her daughters that I should come by quickly to see her before she passed. I immediately rushed to her home. She was on the hospice hospital bed with all sorts of tubes and monitors attached to her, but she gave me the biggest smile as I entered the room. Her daughter indicated she didn't have much energy to talk. I just stood beside her, holding her hand. I had never experienced unconditional love like Elizabeth's. I could clearly see she was very weak. She smiled at me and said, "This is quite the journey. I highly recommend it." I told her I loved her and softly let go of her hand as I said goodbye.

I am reminded of her every time I drive near where she had lived. It isn't a feeling of sadness when I am reminded; rather, it is a feeling of gratitude. She is part of who I am. She is in me. And I am forever changed.

The gift of taking a hard look at how I've affected others and making amends

Family week

Not unlike many families in the last decade, our family, too, was caught unprepared for the onslaught of opiates affecting the lives of our loved ones. My first awareness of it entering our own lives was a call from a local hospital informing me they were treating a family member's overdose. I would become extremely grateful for the lifesaving skills and commitment of the doctors and nurses who saved their life.

As a father and a counselor, I felt shame. Where had I missed seeing this coming? What did I do or not do that caused this? I became focused on "rescuing" them from their drug use with countless interventions of drug treatment programs and treatment centers. It only got worse. I was in chaos; our family was in chaos, and I didn't have a clue how to stop the crazy-making. "I'm supposed to know these things," I told myself.

At one of the family weeks at an inpatient treatment center, I participated not only in counseling sessions with my loved ones, but in family group meetings with other parents and spouses as well. As the week came to an end, a staff member approached me and said, "You need to go to Al-anon."

I was aware of AA and NA and had made referrals in my counseling work. But this referral was for *me*. I arrived at my first meeting ashamed, scared, physically and emotionally exhausted, and unsure what good this Al-anon could do to "save" my loved ones. The answer was "not a thing." Al-anon was about me. I had to come to a point where I recognized I couldn't control or cure them, and I was not the cause of my loved one's addictions.

I also had to learn about myself. I did the 12 steps with the difficult recognition I had some accountability to look at. I needed to take a hard look at how my actions affected others. And I needed to make some amends. I also learned I wasn't alone and found community in people who knew exactly what I was going through and how I felt.

The gift of powerlessness also applied in being able to turn it over to something higher than myself—that if I believed I was able to love my family members, maybe I could trust that they were already loved.

I have been changed by the gift of turning it over, in trusting something higher than myself. My loved ones don't have to deal with someone who is trying to control, to rescue, or to take over. And with that, we are healing together.

Part Two
Reflections

There is pain and suffering that cannot be called an "unexpected gift"

I have shared my experiences and my journey in an attempt to connect with discoveries you may be finding in your own life that were not anticipated, perhaps felt confusing and awful, and yet brought new perspectives, new appreciations, new gratitude that wouldn't have occurred without those "unexpected gifts." Gifts that nudged us into letting go of what actually needed to be let go of and being open to the new and unknown. But now, I come to larger, more universal questions that I have felt completely inadequate to address. I've read many responses and philosophies, explanations, and theories, but none have fully satisfied the question for me. It is the human experience of somehow living with both chaos and order that I am beginning to try to wrap my head around.

If there is meaning in life, why are so many of us left to sheer survival and nothing more? Where's the equity in the "all men" are created equally? How can it be that we are the most destructive and vicious species with our supposed superior brains and technologies? There's no sign of letting up in our destructiveness as the missiles fly faster, grow more powerful, and are ready in a moment's notice to serve our greed and hatred.

I attended a lecture that left all of us in the audience silent as the speaker placed a large metal bowl before us, placed it on a stand, and said, "This is the power of the two nuclear blasts at Hiroshima and Nagasaki." She then proceeded to pour a few BBs into the clanging bowl from a large glass jar.

"Now," she continued, "This is the number of nuclear bombs in the world we have armed and ready to launch today." She began to pour again. But this time, 10 seconds went by, 20 seconds, a minute, 2 minutes. The clanging metal bowl left us horrified and grateful for the end of the clanging BBs.

After reflecting honestly on the reality of our past and current human conditions, I can't avoid the sinking feeling that maybe I am just placating myself, seeking to hold on to those rose-colored glasses as tightly as I can—denying my membership as a certifiable Pollyanna.

What about the "in your face" cruelty, hatred, and unbelievable acts of terror that are a very real part of our world and our lives that we must acknowledge? Where are the gifts in these? What if, in fact, there are "gifts" in life's struggles for some but not all? Is this a dual system where some people get to experience growth and meaning from loss and hardship while others are only left to cruel and unthinkable destinies? That sounds like the very message I so vehemently opposed from my childhood. If your skin is not the right color, if you're not from the right culture, if you're not the right gender, if you're not in the right religion or from the right family, if you're not at the right place at the right time, you go to the back of the bus. And you will suffer.

And that's when I was reminded of a sermon I heard at a Thanksgiving ecumenical service with all the faith traditions joined together. The pastor was a fiery speaker and passionate about his topic: "If you're not receiving God's love, somebody's in the way." He spoke of the concept of a birthright—not the kind of inheriting tents and sheep and cattle of centuries past, but the kind that is needed by every human being.

He noted that the word "baby" is not a singular term, for no baby can survive without a community. He sees the word as a plural—that every one of us needed someone to nurture us, feed us, protect us, guide us, tell us the truth, believe in us, and love us. That is every human being's birthright: for us to be able to Live with a capital L. If we aren't receiving those essentials to human life, someone is in the way—not recognizing that every one of us is precious and worthy of our birthright.

The horrors you and I see in our history books and the daily news are the direct result of the denial and the stripping of our human birthrights. But birthrights can be restored when eyes are opened. Spirituality is about seeing birthrights through eyes of love. That everyone and everything is precious. That life is sacred. *That* is the gift. Any one of us can claim it and be changed by it. Interestingly enough, the results often bring us to becoming more childlike—open, celebrating, laughing more, accepting, playful, noticing the beauty all around us we didn't see before ... all benefits—all unexpected gifts of living a life devoted to restoring birthrights in countless different ways.

The other concept I am reminded of comes from my time volunteering at a homeless shelter in Detroit. The woman in charge of the program was clearly devoted to the people who came through that shelter's front door. At each mealtime, she would offer the blessing. And it would go something like this: "Lord, we know you are here in this room with us today, and we are honored for you to be with us. We hope the food we have prepared for you today will meet your approval. Thank you for being in our midst today and for the privilege of your presence."

She was reminding us of the scripture passage in Matthew 25:40, "Inasmuch as ye have done it unto one of the least of these my brethren, ye have done it to me."

Taken from the view of all we are learning today about the amazing diversity, beauty, intricacy, and complexity of life, how can we not see and feel the awe of being in the presence of something miraculous that moves us to see all life as sacred? To me, that is *the* most precious gift.

Some thoughts on living, giving, and receiving unexpected gifts

I have shared stories in this book about how people from all ages and backgrounds came and went in my life, leaving precious, unexpected gifts with me. I am changed by their words, their actions, their love, their presence, and their departure. Today, and each new day, I seek to offer the same to those who come and go in my life. The following sections are a few gifts I'd like to leave with *you*.

You can never give more than you receive

As your unexpected, unplanned, completely off-course-from-where-I-thought-I-was-going life evolves, chances are good you will be increasingly aware of those who come and go in your life who just might benefit from your presence, empathy, and care. But be warned. This shift in one's worldview comes at a price. You cannot ever, *ever* give more than you receive. It just works that way.

It is a paradox. We know now that our human brains develop from the back to the front. From the "reward center" acting on impulse to the analytical prefrontal cortex carefully weighing pros and cons, good idea or bad idea, maybe I shouldn't do that, and squashing unsafe actions. On the other hand, the reward center works wonderfully in developing early skills from walking to talking to giving us positive reinforcement for making choices that help us survive.

So, doing something "good" in hopes of some kind of "reward," such as getting a raise or a promotion or "going to heaven" is a fairly simplistic, self-serving act. In our being able to witness and respond to human needs, give freely of ourselves out of compassion and kindness, make sacrifices out of a sense of conviction and empathy, we are on a whole different level of human behavior. It comes from awareness.

But, regardless of your other-care focus and even sacrifice, you will benefit. You will feel joy. You will feel connected. It just comes with the territory. You can follow your passion for kindness or justice anonymously. Doesn't matter. You can refuse any recognition of any kind. Doesn't help. So be warned that seeking to offer unexpected gifts to others will just keep on giving back more than you ever imagined. You'll catch yourself smiling a lot, laughing out loud, and just enjoying the moment. Some might say you seem happy.

Don't say I didn't warn you.

People will think you're nuts

When was the last time you made a child giggle? Remember? My three-year-old granddaughter and I used to sit across the table from each other when we would all go out for a family meal. And, inevitably, I couldn't resist the urge to make my best funny face. She not only laughed but immediately returned the favor with her own funny face, which cracked me up. We were on—that is, until Mom caught sight of us at the other end of the table and put our silliness to a stop. But man, three-year-olds are great at making funny faces.

Somehow, the pretense and appropriate behaviors just go out the window when it means giving a child an opportunity to laugh and giggle.

Ever pet a plant? Evidently, research tells us they notice. I have a beautiful fern in my backyard that decided it wanted to live here. Every time I walk by and notice how beautiful it is, I can't resist giving it a "thank you for being so beautiful" petting.

While I was sitting with my family at a nice restaurant, our server accidentally tripped holding a full pitcher of iced tea, pouring it completely over me. There was a moment of sudden silence in the restaurant. The kids took one look at me, and the shocked looks on their faces just made me lose it. I started laughing uncontrollably. Relieved at my reaction, my family started laughing, too. I looked pretty ridiculous soaked head to foot in iced tea. The server brought towels, apologizing again and again, and gave us all free desserts. Years later, we still joke about the free desserts everyone had.

Most of life is about lightness, noticing little things, getting people out of their comfort zones a bit, finding a way for someone who's way too serious to soften for a moment. It is playing the sacred fool.

You are not alone

I'm currently reading a book by William MacAskill entitled, *Doing Good Better*. He notes that altruism is alive and well in our world as many of us choose making a difference as the priority in what we do with our lives.

But there's another dimension to the statement, "You're not alone." It is the realization that love doesn't come from you. It comes *through you.* This is pretty powerful stuff. There are different words or descriptions for this awareness, but somehow, they all seem to fall short. What is exciting for me is to see so many disciplines recognizing they are using different words but are all pointing to the same awareness. Even quantum physicists and Buddhist monks are finding common insights pointing to the same realizations. Words like "consciousness" are taking on new expanded definitions of connection and depth as we learn more about our universe and our brains.

Ever wake up in the middle of the night with an idea you have to get up and write down? As a composer and musician, I thrive on these experiences. My wife has become quite accustomed to my suddenly getting up to jot down chords, melody lines, and draft lyrics. I actually hear the songs in my head.

This experience can hold true for many, many disciplines. Often, you hear of researchers hitting a wall and giving up only to wake to a solution the next morning.

As a spiritual experience, it is sometimes having overwhelming feelings rush over you as you are touched by something powerful, inspiring, beyond words—which leads us to another empowering word.

Empathy.

You and I have this awesome power— it's called empathy

Sometimes it may feel more like a curse than a gift. Empathy, that is. To feel another person's pain and be unable to relieve or heal that pain is hard. Escape can be one of our initial responses. But remaining, standing by, hanging in there, and holding someone's hand is what we are called to do. Hospital patients fare better with someone advocating for and supporting them. But powerlessness is VERY uncomfortable. We feel like we should do more and are frustrated with our lack of ability to do something, *anything* tangible that feels like helping.

It is amazingly healing when someone is with us who truly understands our pain. I have a friend who lost his wife to cancer just before I met him. It was a life-altering event for him. And his first reaction was to bury himself in his work. But he soon realized that was not what he needed to do. He refocused on his kids' need for support and presence, and he became a volunteer at a nearby hospital leading support groups for spouses who had lost their loved one to cancer.

Eventually, he decided to return to school and earn his degree and credentials as a counselor for spouses and families. He still misses his wife every day. But when someone tells him about the confusion and pain they feel, he can fully hear them and be there for them.

Some thoughts on living, giving, and receiving unexpected gifts

You will get pissed off

This is a mixed one for me. So, we have the Scripture story of Jesus coming to the temple and chasing away the money changers and vendors taking advantage of those trying to follow religious law after long journeys to Jerusalem. Jesus didn't just observe the corrupt exploiters; he turned over their tables, made a whip, and drove them out. Archbishop Desmond Tutu speaks of righteous anger when one sees innocent others being harmed. It is anger as a tool for justice. It is a chosen response, not a reflexive response.

I feel that anger. I feel that anger toward those who have flooded our communities with opiates, leading to so many of our loved ones becoming addicts as the perpetrators make huge profits and essentially have little consequences for the unbelievable harm and pain they have caused.

I feel that anger as I am aware of the 450,000 children in the United States in foster care due to so many social problems brought on by institutional racism and the resulting poverty and lack of resources when we live in such a rich country.

But I also hear the Dalai Lama's words of anger coming out of fear. And if we can see the anger coming from fear in others, we have the opportunity to use our rational minds to move toward compassion.

In seeking a life of bringing unexpected gifts, we are voluntarily choosing to see what is unjust, what is cruel, what is exploitive and dehumanizing, and to call it out.

You will be in awe

Robert Sapolsky wrote a brilliantly researched book on human behavior in 2017, appropriately entitled *BEHAVE*. Most of his adult life has been dedicated to defining why we behave the way we do. No surprise; it's complicated. And the large volume covers all the levels—from genetic to neurological, from hormonal to environmental, from heritage to culture, from familial to regional. It is an exhaustive study. He spent many summers observing baboons, noting how various influences predicted behavior. And then he turned to us. Behavior by behavior, he identified the prompts that lead us to act the way we do.

Sapolsky also noted he didn't believe in any kind of "angel on our shoulder" (my term) that could suddenly take over and lead us to "the right choice." For me, the book was both amazingly informative in its depth and a bit depressing. It felt like, ultimately, life is just a train ride to Cleveland as we helplessly ride along. But I know that wasn't his point. I believe Sapolsky was seeking to help us increasingly understand not only ourselves, but life itself.

The reason I refer to his book is that I find myself contemplating many of his points:

1. We are here by accident. Example: the meteor that struck earth and wiped out most of life on our planet.
2. The number of possible paths life could have taken but didn't are in part the result of chance.
3. Why would some all-knowing creator who oversaw billions of years and billions of stars, galaxies, and planets focus on this tiny planet to reveal himself and give us some rules (or else!)?

I can't argue with those points. But I do hold to another maxim as well that is increasingly affirmed: *The universe is predisposed to life.*

We are finding it everywhere we look. In deep sea caves with crushing pressures, potentially in moons of other planets ... We are just getting started in seeing the amazing abundance of life developing in multitudes of environments. And we are seeing increasing examples of life having memory and, therefore, consciousness. Life is evolving, and so are we.

Dorothea Harvey, a Bible scholar at Urbana University, came to her own conclusions as she considered the sacred stories passed on for thousands of years. She began to see a parallel dynamic of individual human evolvement with collective human evolvement. By no means are either in a straight-line path. Both have jumps and starts, two steps forward, three back, going one way then another.

Child development studies carefully identify changes in perception, relationship skills, and awareness as a child grows and evolves.

Sacred texts, according to Harvey, paint a similar picture. God (or creator, parent, authority) is presented as absolute authority with very human moods and behaviors. God gets angry and punishes them, and then later forgives. But, as sacred texts continue and evolve, God is seen as protector and advocate and attentive. God can be argued with. God can rescue. God can lead. God can point to a better future.

In other words, consider the evolving perceptions of a child under the care of a parent. Mom and Dad nurture, set boundaries, punishments, praise successes, promote learning, have to be lied to or get punished, and so on. We individually and collectively are evolving to ever-increasing awareness—as bumpy a road as it is. We are the collective "child" evolving just as the individual child evolves. We have exceptional potential in both being able to be co-creators in the universe and to become increasingly "conscious." Being conscious of the forces within us from our earliest evolvement connects us to everything—from subatomic particles/waves to the very elements from the stars, from mold slime to humpback whales.

And this is where I find awe. Yes, I am my brain. If something happens to my brain, I am changed or consciously gone. But every element, particle, atom remains. I just borrowed them for a while. Perhaps you have heard or read that we breathe the same air that Jesus breathed:

> **From Rees Sloan, *Anavastha*:** "The reality is that the odds of breathing a single molecule of air that once passed through the lungs of Jesus, even in a single one of your breaths, is near certainty. The odds of encountering even one of those molecules within your entire lifetime is even more certain."

Yes, we will die. But we also will remain. Not only in terms of molecules, but in terms of the words and actions we leave behind—the day-to-day differences we made. You and I participate in the dance of creation, the dance of life. As subtle as it may be, we all become one step in life's billions of steps in the universe's predisposition to life. And I am in awe.

Some thoughts on chaos and order

Perhaps you have seen the symbol of the yin and yang, light and darkness with darkness at the center of light and light at the center of darkness. It is an image of balance, of change, of chaos at the center of order, order at the center of chaos. The combined energies of evolving life.

We need both—learning to live like that farmer mentioned at the beginning of this book, without judgment, accepting what comes with openness and moving on with life. Unexpected gifts can teach us to be open to the possibilities in life; to be aware of something deeper and more meaningful than we ever realized before.

I was struck by a statement by an astronomer who observed that the universe needed to evolve the billions of years it has existed before we could exist—the generations of countless stars forming, expanding, and exploding, sending ever more complex elements throughout the universe, the gravitational pulls of galaxies on galaxies, stars on stars, planets on planets, creating collisions and reformations until equilibrium and stability could occur, the ever-evolving levels of life from particles to elements to molecules to cells to vegetation to us!

Are we the ultimate end of the universe? Or are we a part of something yet to be seen beyond ourselves? Are we stewards of the future?

One thing I do believe is we've underestimated the wonder, the looking up to what might yet be possible because we have yet to fully open our eyes to the countless gifts all around us in every moment. Remember the woman who asked, "Who is invisible to you?" Maybe the question to add is, "*What* is invisible to you?"

Instead of seeing others as unexpected gifts in our lives, I am proposing to take that one step further and consider that *we* are and always have been the *expected* gift all along. We are here because we are loved. We are a part of—and co-creators in—what is yet to come. We belong. We are connected in ways beyond our imaginations.

I have come to love sailing with a passion and am out on the water every chance I get. It is a spiritual thing for me. When I am out sailing, I feel calm and peaceful, but also quite playful and adventurous. It is an all-absorbing interplay between what I have control of and what I do not have control of. I set my sails and adapt to the wind. And suddenly, unpredictably, it shifts, and I am forced to make quick changes. Or I can find myself in a very boring, windless drift as I wait for the next breeze. It is a give and take in the moment. I think of nothing else but the wind and my response to it. The more I sail and practice, the better I get. I extend my boundaries and try new waters and discover new beauty I would not have seen otherwise. I am fully engaged.

That is how I see life in so many ways. It's a lot of practice. Mistakes are painful. Hoping for something better can take a while. It requires us to be open to possibilities. It introduces us to beauty we would never have seen if we hadn't learned how to navigate new waters and try new adventures. It's about engaging fully.

May the stories and thoughts I've shared from my life be of use in sharing the beauty and wonder of your life with someone else. May *you* be an unexpected gift.

PSALM 139:1-18 (ESV)

For the director of music. Of David. A psalm.

O LORD, you have searched me and known me!
² You know when I sit down and when I rise up;
you discern my thoughts from afar.
³ You search out my path and my lying down
and are acquainted with all my ways.
⁴ Even before a word is on my tongue,
behold, O LORD, you know it altogether.
⁵ You hem me in, behind and before,
and lay your hand upon me.
⁶ Such knowledge is too wonderful for me;
it is high; I cannot attain it.
⁷ Where shall I go from your Spirit?
Or where shall I flee from your presence?
⁸ If I ascend to heaven, you are there!
If I make my bed in Sheol, you are there!
⁹ If I take the wings of the morning
and dwell in the uttermost parts of the sea,

[10] even there your hand shall lead me,
and your right hand shall hold me.
[11] If I say, "Surely the darkness shall cover me,
and the light about me be night,"
[12] even the darkness is not dark to you;
the night is bright as the day,
for darkness is as light with you.
[13] For you formed my inward parts;
you knitted me together in my mother's womb.
[14] I praise you, for I am fearfully and wonderfully made.
Wonderful are your works;
my soul knows it very well.
[15] My frame was not hidden from you,
when I was being made in secret,
intricately woven in the depths of the earth.
[16] Your eyes saw my unformed substance;
in your book were written, every one of them,
the days that were formed for me,
when as yet there was none of them.
[17] How precious to me are your thoughts, O God!
How vast is the sum of them!
[18] If I would count them, they are more than the sand.
I awake, and I am still with you.

ABOUT THE AUTHOR

Stephen Now is a licensed mental health therapist (LMHC) and an ordained chaplain with over 30 years providing counseling and support to families and children. He has served as an emergency center and pediatric intensive care chaplain, as a therapist for children and youth in treatment foster care and as clinical supervisor of a community youth and family services center.

He has volunteered for many years supporting moms and children living in family shelters and as a Court Appointed Special Advocate (CASA) for children in social services and foster care. He currently serves on the program committee of Treehouse Foundation providing resources and support for foster youth through age 26 ensuring every possibility for their having a sustainable adult life through education, mentoring and financial support.

Stephen has often used his background in music and theatre to bring opportunities for those he counsels to find new ways of expression and meaning.

www.ingramcontent.com/pod-product-compliance
Lightning Source LLC
LaVergne TN
LVHW041637060526
838200LV00040B/1611